COMMUNICATION BREAKTHROUGH

HOW USING BRAIN SCIENCE AND LISTENING TO BODY CUES CAN TRANSFORM YOUR RELATIONSHIPS

Vincentia Schroeter, PhD

Wolfheart Press
Alpine, CA

Schroeter/Wolfheart Press
Alpine, CA

Communication Breakthrough/Schroeter. -- 1st ed.
ISBN 978-0996324953

Dedication

I dedicate this book to my beloved husband, Steve, who rescues me when computers get beyond my skill level, listens compassionately to my ups and downs, believes in me and has gently offered the perfect balance of close contact and personal space in our union for over thirty-five years.

Communication is a skill that you can learn. It's like riding a bicycle or typing. If you're willing to work at it, you can rapidly improve the quality of every part of your life.

~Brian Tracy

Contents

Introduction

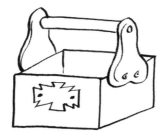

HAVE YOU ever felt as if you were speaking to someone, being as clear as a bell, yet the other person
simply didn't understand your point?

You know the conversation I'm talking about—when
you're sure you've made your needs clear, yet the other person
appears angry, distracted or trapped. Then in turn, you find
yourself feeling annoyed, lonely or lost.

At a moment like that, you may be wondering:

Why doesn't s/he understand what I'm saying?

Why don't they get what I need?

Why can't I make myself heard?

1

The goal of this book is to end those complaints. Using the latest in brain research and body psychotherapy, my goal is to share with you tools that are both practical and life changing. You'll find yourself awakened as a better listener and more skillful as a communicator.

Why doesn't s/he get what I'm saying? becomes *It feels so good to be heard and understood.*

Why don't they get what I need? becomes *I stated my needs clearly.*

Why can't I make myself be heard? becomes *I reached out and now I have support.*

WHO MIGHT BENEFIT FROM THIS BOOK:

- Husbands and wives struggling to be heard
- Parents frustrated at not getting through to their children
- Singles attempting to maneuver in the dating world
- Co-workers seeking to reduce confusion or conflicts
- Sons or daughters wanting to feel heard by their parents
- Employees or bosses seeking to create a culture of healthy communication
- Those who want to brush up on their communication skills or add a few new ones to their tool box

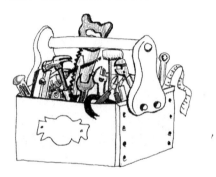

My Background

I received a Master's degree in Clinical Psychology from the University of San Francisco and was licensed as a Marriage and Family Therapist in 1975. I've worked in clinics, a halfway house for women prisoners, a residential treatment center for autistic children, a treatment center for male alcoholics and a group therapy center for convicted drunk drivers. I helped form and was the director of a day treatment center for women alcoholics and their children, the first one of its kind in San Francisco. I've had a private practice and was trained as an addictions specialist and group therapist.

I found my way to the method that would become my primary approach—Bioenergetics—in 1980 when I became a Certified Bioenergetic Analyst (CBT.) Bioenergetics is a form of psychotherapy that sees how emotional struggles are manifest in the muscular holdings of the body and provides somatic techniques (such as breathing and grounding) to better manage those struggles. In 1999, I received a PhD in Clinical Psychology, doing research on mother and infant bonding with an interest in the interplay of nature and nurture in the development of attachment. I had a private practice for 10 years in San Francisco, then another 32 years in San Diego working with families, couples, children and individuals.

I served as an adjunct professor at San Francisco State on the dynamics of group therapy and taught doctor-patient communication skills at PCOM (Pacific College of Oriental Medicine) for 13 years. I'm currently on the International faculty for the IIBA (International Institute for Bioenergetic Analysis), as well as chief editor of the IIBA journal, Bioenergetic Analysis, (2008-2018).

In all these roles, I've been determined to hone my skills at finding the best communication techniques for the job— whether teaching a workshop in Hong Kong or Spain, counseling a family in conflict or reaching out to help a distraught mother, angry teenager, depressed father or shy student in my practice.

HOW TO USE THIS BOOK

Chapter One provides an overview of the whole book, so you can get a good feeling for the journey on which you're about to embark. In Chapter Two, I'll provide you with two self-assessment tools (on listening and assertiveness) as keys to learning about your communication style. The rest of the book offers unique Mind/Body tools that will enhance communication with effective aids for better listening and more effective expression. The final chapter focuses solely on applying these tools in crisis situations including grief, breakups, anger management, sadness management and emergency room protocol. You can skip around in the book or proceed chapter by chapter. In completing each section in order, you'll maximize the benefits of the book by learning the most tools, as they're presented in a progressive manner.

DISCLAIMER: The stories I share in this book are based on my experiences or those of clients I've treated in my counseling practice. Identities have been altered to protect the confidentiality of my clients. Any advice given in this book should not be a substitute for the professional advice or treatment a psychologist, psychiatrist, health care provider or licensed mental health counselor would give to an actual client in his or her care.

Wondering how it all works? Let's take a look.

Sam and the Volcano Zone

A few years back Sam and Nora came in for marriage counseling. Well, in truth, Sam was hoping to save the marriage and Nora was hoping that counseling could help them separate in the most peaceful way possible. She felt exhausted by their short five-year marriage and thought Sam's anger was something he would never be able to control. Together they had a rambunctious and sweet four-year-old boy named Jared. In the first session Nora revealed a shocking secret to Sam. She had already filed for divorce and waited to tell Sam because she was afraid he might explode. Sam was visibly crushed. He broke down and stated that he desperately wanted to save their marriage and felt that Nora was the love of his life. Furthermore he had grown up in a broken home, traveling between two households and didn't want that fate for their son.

Nora and Sam both worked from home while Jared was in preschool. They were trying to launch an online business and finances were tight. When Nora would discuss what wasn't going right in the family business, she said Sam would often fly into a rage. Nora said she felt as if she was living in terror. She said she couldn't always tell what was going on inside Sam and sometimes what looked like simple frustration escalated into what she called "The Volcano Zone." This was where Sam would swear and curse and lash out at Nora (and sometimes their son). The tirades could last up to 30 minutes and Nora said that Sam was completely unreachable once he was that outraged. Nora would experience depression and hopelessness and oftentimes they wouldn't be able to get any work done. This only compounded their financial difficulties. Since early on in the marriage Nora had told Sam he had an anger problem and being told this only seemed to make him more frustrated. He hated being labeled that way. I asked them to put the divorce talk and the labeling talk on hold to see if we might be able to use some concrete communication tools. I first taught them what happens to someone's brain when they're experiencing rage. This helped Nora because she could better understand what was going on inside Sam and how he was experiencing a sense of being out of control. This helped Sam because he began to see that there was a neurological response occurring inside of him.

We next talked over the tool that you'll read in Chapter Four called "Standing Down." I explained to Sam and Nora that Standing Down is a simple technique that helps you walk away from a tense situation that might escalate and get out of control. We talked about creating a standing down plan so both Nora and Sam would feel empowered, so they would know what to do if Sam was heading toward the volcano zone. Sam said he was able to notice he was getting into the volcano zone when his jaw clenched and his fists balled up. The moment he felt his body "talking to him" in this way he could implement his standing down plan. In the next session we developed...

Sam's Standing Down Plan

When Sam noticed cues in his body (fists clenching, jaw tightening) Sam would tell Nora, "I think I'm hitting the volcano zone." Once he expressed that they both knew what to do. Nora's job was to remove herself and spend some time alone working or going for a walk. Sam's job was to stop talking all together, get completely silent and go into the garage. He created a place for himself in the garage where he could decompress. He would sit on his workbench, place his feet firmly on the floor and take five deep breaths. Sometimes he would sit quietly and then take five more. During the first few breaths he often found that he was still cursing and muttering to himself about what was making him angry. Sam shared that usually by the fifth breath the inner dialogue had ceased. After he finished his deep breathing, Sam might do some tinkering with one of his woodworking projects. The whole process usually took about 30 minutes.

At that point the couple would text each other and be able to resume their discussion. More often than not they were able to return to work and have a productive day. Within three months, standing down was just part of their routine and they even began teaching it to their son. Nora expressed great joy at having found a way to revive the marriage and Sam was relieved to have found a lifeline in what he felt was an easy life tool.

What communication tool might come to the rescue and provide the life vest for you?

BETTER COMMUNICATION = A BETTER LIFE!

NOTE: *How do you know when a self-help book is not enough help?*
This book is designed as a practical aid to improve communication skills in a way that can be used by almost anyone. However, while a book like this can provide skills that improve your life, it may not feel like enough to make you as happy as you wish to be. When you feel a level of discontent that isn't shifting, even when you try the tools in the book, then the book isn't enough. If you're struggling emotionally you may benefit from having someone to talk to who can guide you on the road to a happier life. In this case a psychotherapist who listens and provides space for you to explore your issues can be very beneficial. Also, if you're in therapy, a book like this can be an aid as you work on issues related to improving communication skills.

CHAPTER ONE

Your Hard-Wired Brain and Talking Body Help Communication

In this first chapter, I start with sharing that good communication is two-pronged, involving both effective speaking as well as active listening. Next I introduce you to the part of brain science that shows how calming the brain leads to the most effective communication. Then I'll tell you about Bioenergetics and how to use your body cues to shift moods for optimum communication.

What does it mean to give and take?
While this may sound obvious, good communication involves the give and take of talking to others. It's necessary to *give* in terms of speaking in a style that clearly communicates your intentions. It's also necessary to *take* in terms of being an active listener, attentively receptive to the messages of the speaker.

Over my 40 years as a psychotherapist I've seen that difficulties in communication can cause major problems for individuals, couples, families and businesses. The following are common examples of declarations I've often heard in my office:

- "You don't understand me!" a teen screams at his parents.
- "How can I get through to you?" a parent begs of her child.
- "Just don't worry about it so much. It will be okay," a husband (whose intention is to be reassuring) answers dismissively.
- "If you knew me, you'd know what I need," a wife implores (expecting mind-reading from her spouse).

I've seen so many people suffer emotionally because they've never been taught basic communication skills. Much of this suffering comes from an inability to express themselves and therefore to be understood by others. Frustration may lead to feeling threatened and then to lashing out. Lashing out reveals the anger and hurt that's beneath the pain of not being understood. *Why is the feeling of being misunderstood so common?* The answer lies in the fact that most of us aren't taught at home or in school:

- How to truly sit back and listen to another human being.
- How to clearly communicate ideas, feelings or needs.
- How to skillfully manage our emotions or moods (which can greatly help or hinder communication).

The Good News

I've found many techniques through the years that can be a bridge over the chasm of isolation created by a failure in communication. I've integrated a newer understanding of the brain and body to help you apply these skills. I've chosen the tools that can be used by most people as they're generally easy to apply. And with just a bit of self-exploration and practice you can master these spirit-lifting communication tools.

You can do it!

Being Wired to Survive: Three Colors That Can Change the Way You Think

Red (LIKE THE COLOR OF A STOP SIGN)

- Fight
- Flight

Green (LIKE THE COLOR OF A TREE)

- Calm
- Engaged

Blue (LIKE THE COLOR OF THE OCEAN)

- Trapped
- Depressed

I'm excited to bring you information from the latest understanding of how the brain affects the nervous system. It comes from the field of interpersonal neurobiology, specifically The Polyvagal Theory created by Stephen Porges (2011). Porges explains that we're wired to survive as a species by automatically assessing safety or danger. The "poly" refers to three states we go into. The zone color concept was created by Daniel Siegel and Tina Payne Bryson (2011). Check the resources by chapter at the end of the book. These are the three states:

1. When feeling safe we're in the **first** state and can communicate calmly from integrated feelings and thoughts. I call this the GREEN ZONE as it's the ideal mindset for effective communication.

2. When we sense danger we first try to fight or withdraw. Anger or fear may escalate. That's the **second** state. I call this the RED ZONE where our fear or anger rises and it can rise so high that we flip our lid in rage or run away.

3. If that fails and we still can't get through to someone or we feel trapped like there's no way out, we enter the **third** state and collapse into depression, hopelessness or a frozen state. This is where we might space out so we can feel less trapped. I call this the BLUE ZONE for the sense of cold immobilization. The best words can't come to mind when we're in this protective state.

Our human brain is wired to react in this order (GREEN, RED then BLUE) when we attempt communication. Later in this book we'll revisit these three zones with techniques to manage the RED and BLUE zones and techniques to return to and stay longer in the GREEN zone.

We'll be using the RED, GREEN and BLUE zones throughout the book in presenting communication techniques.

Where the Body Fits In

Bioenergetics is a mind/body psychotherapy that I've been practicing for 40 years. It was created by Alexander Lowen in 1956 and helps people connect to their body states. Here's how it works. When we're stressed each of us tends to carry tension somewhere in our body. For example, some people get headaches while others feel stress in their shoulders, necks or stomachs. But even when we're not stressed we often carry ourselves in restricted ways. These are called "chronic tension patterns." Have you ever seen someone walking down the street looking scared with raised shoulders even though there was no danger? Or someone looking tough with a stern look and arms that look ready for a fight? Why? Well those folks walk around that way all the time. It's like they're stuck in those poses. Their body stance both expresses who they are and protects them from their view of danger. So the scared-looking person who keeps his shoulders up and eyes wide open for signs of danger has often had to cope with hostility and rejection. From his childhood experience he learned that keeping alert and withdrawn is safer than being relaxed and trusting. That was the best way to adapt to his family. Same for the strong ready-to-fight looking person. Being able to take care of herself and appear tough was the best stance in her family. So these patterns helped us cope in the past but now as adults they also limit our openness.

People who come to Bioenergetic therapy work to change those patterns, not just by understanding their origin, but also by doing movement exercises that help them gain back more flexibility of expression. So the scared person can work to relax those shoulders and eyes, while working on trust with an empathic therapist and the strong ready to fight person can work to soften her arms and face, while working on being vulnerable with an understanding therapist. We'll use some of this knowledge of body tension patterns in our work in this book.

Believe it or not, these patterns also interfere with communication. Looking at communication through a Bioenergetics lens can help us to:

- Shift breathing patterns to change mood and enhance communication.
- Locate in the body and mobilize feelings that can improve communication.
- Center and de-escalate from overreacting with anger.
- Stand up for ourselves when needed.

Open the Door

Good communication opens doors to the heart and to your often-hidden true self. Learning good communication is like pushing that barely open door further ajar, allowing you to better understand others and hopefully to let others in to see the real you. Bringing the authentic, vulnerable, honest you into the light (even though you may carry some shame or guilt) is what makes you best understood and as a result most beloved by others.

Together, let's open the door and walk toward a better understanding of you and others. Let's break down the myths, pick up some new tools and improve communication and in turn, your daily life.

Take Aways:

1. Good communication involves both speaking and listening skills that are rarely taught in homes or schools.
2. Most people have been victims and perpetrators of poor communication and know the pain of being misunderstood.
3. The calm brain in the GREEN ZONE is the most effective communicator.

4. Breathing and centering techniques help the body communicate effectively.

5. Communication skills that can enhance joy in life can be learned.

CHAPTER TWO

Listening Blocks and Assertiveness Issues That Get in Your Way

In Chapter One, I discussed how effective communication involves a give and take. We're now going to dive a bit deeper into the give and take of powerful communication. I'm going to give you two simple (though not always easy) keys to getting heard and truly hearing others.

Two Valuable Keys of Communication
The keys are:

1. Becoming Aware of Your Listening Blocks
2. Expressing Yourself Assertively

KEY #1: Become Aware of Listening Blocks

The first key involves becoming aware of blocks you may be using so you're not fully hearing or understanding the person speaking. Think of these blocks like your own personal earmuffs. You can selectively choose what and how you hear with your earmuffs and believe it or not you have most likely been doing so for years.

We all have some listening blocks or times we place those earmuffs on. Before exploring the blocks we use, let's read a story about two co-owners whose communication problems threatened to ruin their business.

Laura and Deirdre's Story

Laura and Deirdre were co-owners of a handbag business. They were each the sole support for their families and were fierce hardworking women. They met in business school, became fast friends and for two years they worked incredibly well together. They attributed their success to the fact that they each brought unique strengths to the business. Laura was the behind the scenes designer and Deirdre was the saleswoman and the face of the business.

Deirdre was a sharp New Yorker and considered herself a powerful and convincing communicator. She was an upfront in your face kind of woman who could outshout any person to prove her point. When there was something she didn't like she let it be known. When she saw someone struggling she told him or her how to fix the problem.

Laura was the opposite; she was a polite Midwestern girl who had always considered herself a good listener and creative thinker. She very much disliked conflict and tended not to deal with issues face to face if she could help it.

Laura joked about a time that a pushy woman walked into their shop stating that she hated all handbags. Laura retreated to the back room to finish a design thinking that Deirdre would politely get rid of the rude customer within a few minutes.

When Laura heard laughing coming from the front of the shop she came out and was astonished to see that Deirdre had found the customer a handbag she loved and was walking away happily satisfied.

One thing was clear to both women. When the partnership was going well the business was soaring. But over the last few months their communication had broken down and they found themselves at cross purposes. When they were in tough meetings Laura tended to retreat inside her mind. Deirdre accused her of not listening when she was speaking. Laura accused Deirdre of being overly pushy and demanding. The business was hurting. Sales were sagging.

They decided they would have to meet, just the two of them, to get to the bottom of the problem between them. Their meeting lasted 10 minutes and ended with shouts of "maybe we should disband the business" and "I just can't get through to you no matter what I do." This is where they were when they came to my office.

I sat down with Laura and Deirdre and talked to them about the two valuable keys that could help them with their communication struggles.

What are Listening Blocks?

"I did tell you; you just weren't listening. You never listen to me."

Have you ever been there? Your spouse, co-worker or child tells you they were never told information that you clearly remember telling them? Even more frustrating, you know that often they only half listen and that you rarely get 100% of their attention when you speak.

Chances are though that they might report the exact same experience with you (that you never listen). But how can that be? you may wonder. Is it possible that we're sometimes deaf to what others are trying to communicate? Is it possible that they're deaf to what we have to say? The answer is YES! The reason is because we all employ (at one time or another) those personal earmuffs—otherwise called listening blocks—as a habit.

At the end of this section on listening blocks you'll receive a KEY#1 practical tool to use to combat a favorite listening block during a conversation!

Let's take a step back and think about why we even want to communicate in the first place. Real listening is based on the intention to do one of four things:

1. Understand someone
2. Enjoy someone
3. Learn something
4. Give help or solace

Any need not listed here is **pseudo-listening** which happens when you're waiting for your turn to talk or half-listening to be nice. We're all guilty of pseudo-listening from time to time.

Remember that it's much easier to see the listening blocks others utilize. But everyone uses some listening blocks sometimes and you may even use different ones with different people. The first step is to learn what kind of listening blocks or earmuffs you use. Don't feel bad about identifying these not-so-great communication pitfalls. First of all, give yourself a break; you may have created the blocks during childhood to navigate the not-so-great communicators you encountered. Second, identifying your habits is an empowering step. Knowing the pitfalls you habitually fall into that result in poor listening means you have control toward fixing your communication issues.

Take a moment to circle the listening blocks you use from the list below.

List of Listening Blocks

1. Comparing (deciding who is smarter, more competent, more popular, etc.)
2. Mind Reading (not paying attention to words and thinking you can read people without having to listen to them)
3. Rehearsing (looking interested but really preparing what you want to say)
4. Filtering (listening for some things and not others, e.g. are they angry at me?)
5. Judging (either pre-judging the speaker or what they say and attaching a negative label which makes you stop listening before you've heard them out)
6. Dreaming (paying attention to only a fraction as your mind wanders elsewhere)
7. Identifying (you identify and can't wait to tell your similar story)
8. Advising (jumping in with unsolicited advice; wanting to fix the problem)
9. Sparring (listening long enough to disagree then assert your opinion; includes sarcasm and put-downs; argue and debate)
10. Being Right (proving you're right including lying, shouting, twisting facts, changing the subject, making excuses and accusing)
11. Derailing (changing the subject or making a joke whenever you're bored or uncomfortable with the conversation)

12. Placating (concerned with being nice, agreeable or liked so you don't really listen and you agree with everything being said)

Laura and Deirdre Take on Key #1 (Become Aware of Listening Blocks)

I asked Laura and Deirdre to look at the list of 12 listening blocks to see if they could identify which blocks they might be unconsciously employing. Laura could identify that when Deirdre got a little loud in a meeting Laura would, "put on earmuffs that allowed her to filter and dream." Laura admitted she would pay attention to the issues she agreed with Deirdre on (for example, marketing and promotion). She would filter and sometimes completely ignore the issues she didn't agree with Deirdre on (such as making changes to their product line). Laura also realized that she learned how to use daydreaming and filtering with her father who tended to be overbearing during her childhood. When her father yelled Laura would retreat to a calmer space in her head.

At first, Deirdre could only see Laura's listening blocks and felt she didn't employ any herself. But after further discussion and some specific examples from Laura, Deirdre realized she used Being Right and Advising. Deirdre was shocked to realize that the way she was communicating wasn't effective or helpful. She thought it was the healthy thing to do, to explain and prove why she was right no matter how loud she got. She grew up in a loud expressive family and that's how all her siblings made their points. She also thought she was being helpful when she was giving Laura unsolicited advice. Deirdre was confused how sometimes her loud and expressive personality was effective, say in selling, but not effective for their business partnership. She decided to look at how she might be able to modulate her fiery and feisty way of being in the world.

New counselors' most common listening block

While teaching students who were learning to be counselors one of the most common listening blocks the teachers noticed in the students was Advising. This is to be expected because when we get anxious we want to be helpful, so a natural inclination is to jump in with advice without fully listening. Also, the speaker may be complaining and as your heart goes out to them you're eager to jump in and help. But this good intention is not always useful. How can you know if they really want advice? Maybe all they really need at the moment is to feel heard. The bottom line is that unless someone asks directly for advice and waits for your answer they're probably not seeking advice. They just need to be heard!

I asked the students to notice that when they felt eager to give advice they should just take a few breaths, wait, then look at the speaker and sense if the person was done talking. In order to help students to avoid this common pitfall I would write the following symbol on the whiteboard.

KEY #1: Tool

To combat a listening block think, "Oh, there it is again."

Take some time to honestly examine which listening blocks you use. Once you're aware, the next time you feel an impulse to put those earmuffs over your ears you'll be able to take a step back and say, "Oh, there it is again."

To make this tool the most effective I recommend you pause, take a few breaths and wait. Focus your attention on the speaker. Be aware of being open to taking in what's being said with no other goal.

HOMEWORK: Pick one of your listening blocks and think of a person you use it with. The next time you talk to that person prepare by being aware of your "go to" block and your intention to not use it. Breathe and pause when you feel pulled to use the block. Lean in with your ears and concentrate on listening without using your block. Sense your block fading into the background.

Practicing "Oh, there it is again" will be easier at some points than others but take heart; with time you can improve. The success will show as you begin to delay the automatic use of your block, use it less and eventually (ideally) not use it at all

KEY #2: Expressing Yourself Assertively

The next task on our list is to look at assertiveness. This second key involves learning how to express yourself so you're clear and firm but not aggressive. It involves finding that stable core within and learning how to assert your wants and needs from a calm yet solid place of strength.

Assertiveness speaks to how comfortable you feel about stating your needs simply and clearly. To better understand your comfort level with assertiveness as well as your feelings towards owning your needs take the assertiveness quiz below.

ASSERTIVENESS QUIZ

Use the scale below to assign a number to each item. Place the number after the item. Total your score at the end.

Always   5   4   3   2   1   Never

1. My needs are as important as those of others and I'm entitled to have my needs met.
2. I can ask for help without feeling anxious or guilty.
3. I'm comfortable standing up for myself.
4. I can speak up in a big group with ease.
5. I'm clear about what I want others to do and can express my needs to them.
6. I can easily turn people down and say "no" when I don't want to do what they ask me to do.
7. I confidently express my honest opinion to authority figures.
8. When I experience strong feelings (anger, fear, sadness, hurt), I can verbalize them easily.
9. I enjoy meeting new people and am aware of considering their needs as well as my own in interactions.
10. I own and can express my feelings and don't blame others or put them down when we disagree.

TOTAL SCORE_____

HOW ASSERTIVE ARE YOU?

Scoring:

If your total is 40, or higher you're consistently assertive and handle most situations well.

If your total is 25-40, you're fairly assertive and can improve through practice.

If your total is 10-25, you may be assertive in some situations but your natural reaction is passive or aggressive.

If your total is below 10, you have difficulty being assertive.

A second way of assessing your assertiveness is to look at where you may land on the assertiveness continuum. Yes, there's actually a continuum when asserting your feelings, points of view and needs. One way to think about how people behave on the scale is to measure how much they **value goals versus relationships**. It seems like we all value both, however we each tend, particularly when stressed, to veer toward one side or the other. We either lose ourselves and defer to others or become bossy and push our weight around.

THE ASSERTIVENESS CONTINUUM

PASSIVE----------ASSERTIVE------------AGGRESSIVE

Where does your typical behavior fit on the scale above? How about when you get angry or stressed out?

The following is a story that will illustrate the three styles of response and how they reflect the importance of relationships versus goals.

STRESS AT THE GAS STATION

Here's the scenario: You drive up to a gas station noticing it has only one working gas pump. You pull up behind another car and wait for the person to finish getting his gas so you can fill up. After he finishes he keeps his car at the pump and goes into the mini-market. He's gone about 10 minutes, returns with snacks and sits in his car eating and talking on his cell phone.

Here are possible scenarios for each type:

A. PASSIVE B. ASSERTIVE C. AGGRESSIVE

A. PASSIVE RESPONSE

First you wait patiently. When he returns with snacks, you assume he'll move his car so you can get gas, but he doesn't. You wait patiently for the customer to leave but may begin to feel agitated. You keep waiting until he leaves or you drive around him and leave for another gas station after 20 minutes.

C. AGGRESSIVE RESPONSE

You honk your horn when he goes into the store because he didn't move his car after getting gas. He ignores you. You follow him into the store to demand he move his car but he's in the bathroom. You knock loudly on the bathroom door yelling, "Hey, you selfish creep, get out here and move your car!" When he comes out you're at his car yelling at him until he drives away.

B. ASSERTIVE RESPONSE

You watch to assess what's likely going on. When the customer finishes getting gas but leaves his car at the pump you guess that perhaps he had to pay inside the store. After 10 minutes, you begin feeling annoyed. He climbs into his car carrying snacks and chats on his phone without moving his car. You take a breath and think, which tells you that you wish to take action. You walk up to his window and say,

(FACTS): "Excuse me, I noticed you already filled up. This is the only working pump and I've been waiting 10 minutes."

(NEED): "Please move your car."

He apologizes for being insensitive and quickly pulls his car away.

Let's take a moment to dive deeper into each response on the continuum. While it's true we can behave in all three styles, people have a tendency toward one way or the other most of the time, especially under stress.

PASSIVE: People who often behave passively value their relationships over their individual goals. To keep peace or please others, passive people tend to not speak up for their needs. They either withhold their views or express themselves so indirectly that their meaning is unclear to others. They might mumble, ramble, be vague or speak too softly. They may give in and not assert their needs for fear of hurting or offending someone or just to be nice. However, then they don't get what they want and usually end up frustrated. The good news is that people who are passive are often well liked for being nice. An advantage is that they don't have to take responsibility for decisions and can avoid the risks associated with taking a personal stand. The bad news is that when people are passive others may not know what they need or may walk all over them. They can find themselves becoming a doormat, meeting other's goals and never their own. For example, in the previous story the passive customer never got their gas at that station.

AGGRESSIVE: People who behave aggressively are interested in meeting their goals at the expense of relationships. They walk all over others to get what they want. They're willing to bully, trick, manipulate or hurt others to meet their own needs. Their anger tends to flare quickly so when they don't get their way they blame and attack others by being critical or going into a rage. The good news is they find it easy to express their opinions, feelings and wants. Others often give in and as a result aggressive people often accomplish much in terms of goals and may become quite successful and contribute to the world using their aggression. The bad news is they hurt others to meet these goals and they can be ruthless and abusive, which drives others away. (For example, in the story the aggressive customer name-called and was mean before considering other options).

ASSERTIVE: People who are assertive consider their goals and relationship needs EQUALLY. They weigh their goals against the needs of others in their life. They believe in mutual respect. They're able to speak up for their needs without hurting others. In the assertive mode you can defend yourself, listen to others, ask for what you want and set limits. You can take compliments and respond firmly to criticism. The good news is others understand you because you **communicate clearly and respectfully**. Also, your life is less stressful when you express your thoughts and needs assertively. There's no bad news for being assertive. (For example, in the previous story, the assertive customer assessed both what the other driver might be going through, their own goals, and checked in with their body before acting.)

Normal fluctuations on the continuum

We all go through different moods in a day. It's normal that moods caused by stressors such as hunger, illness, anger, loneliness or being overwhelmed can push us toward one or the other end of the continuum (too passive or too aggressive) whereas when we're rested, well-fed and less stressed we go more toward the middle (assertiveness). Even so, we generally favor more passive or aggressive styles in our personality. If you think of people you know you may notice how some are naturally more aggressive or passive. *What about you?*

Deirdre and Laura on Key #2 (Expressing Yourself Assertively)

Deirdre and Laura each took the assertiveness quiz. Deirdre wasn't shocked to find out that she ranked as aggressive. She was however a little shocked to realize she could be assertive without being aggressive. It was a new idea for her that she could state her wants and needs with strength and not be overpowering.

Laura knew she was more on the passive side but she too was a little shocked at how passive she was in most situations with Deirdre. On the Assertiveness Continuum Scale Laura identified herself as being nowhere near assertive. When I discussed the gas station example, Deirdre and Laura laughed as they could both see Deirdre honking that horn until someone took notice, while Laura would slip inside the gas station bathroom and hide until the conflict was over.

Using what they learned about the listening blocks that they employed, the two cofounders learned to slow down when their communication got rough. They would consciously stop and say, "Oh, there it is again," then be as present as possible. They stated that this helped them to have longer conversations which helped them to talk through some difficult decisions. But what really cracked open their communication issues was that each one declared they would move away from their respective places on the assertiveness continuum and more toward the middle place of being assertive. *How did they do that?* (Here's the assertive scale once more.)

THE ASSERTIVENESS CONTINUUM

PASSIVE------ASSERTIVE------AGGRESSIVE

During a rough conversation when Deirdre noticed she was getting loud and aggressive she would take three deep breaths. She would write down the points she wanted to make sure she got across and give them to Laura in written form. That way she was still being clear as to what she wanted to communicate but she wasn't bullying Laura into some sort of response. When Laura noticed she was getting overly quiet and diving into full passivity she would employ the tool of "Oh, there it is again." She decided she would politely remind Deirdre that she was starting to retreat and she needed Deirdre to speak in a lower calmer voice. She loved the idea of getting Deirdre's thoughts on paper as it allowed her time to think. She said she was still scared when she had to state her opposing thoughts to Deirdre but that Deirdre was allowing her more space and was practicing being assertive. Within a few months of becoming aware and employing their new tools, business started to ramp up again and sales began to soar.

KEY #2: TOOL

I Can Move to the Middle

The next time you're faced with a difficult situation where you feel your needs aren't being met or that you're being disrespected, notice your tendency. Do you want to shrink away and hide? Do you find yourself thinking, "Oh, it doesn't matter that much. I'll just let it go"?

Or do you notice yourself wanting to move forward into a confrontation? Do you find yourself thinking, "They can't do this to me. I better get loud here to make sure they know they're wrong"?

Once you feel which way you're pulled (to shrink back or plunge forward) try this: Stand and press your feet firmly on the floor placing your weight evenly on both feet. Next, rock forward and back on your feet and take a few belly breaths until you find yourself centered in the middle. Pause here with your weight centered. Now from this place how might you respond? Moving to the middle in your body may help you feel the center and therefore be more assertive. How? You will move far enough forward to counteract your tendency to lean back into passivity if you're a passive type. You will move further back to counteract your tendency to lean forward to be aggressive if you're naturally an aggressive type.

Am I too aggressive or too passive? Here's a summary of how to tell if you're usually too passive or aggressive.

Aggressive: I can get my way and get a lot done but I'm impatient, impulsive and willing to plow over others to meet my goals. I'm too aggressive if people often end up hurt by my actions.

Passive: I value kindness toward others but often put others before myself, have difficulty saying "no" or sticking up for myself and tend to be compliant. I'm too passive if I let people walk all over me at times because I believe others' needs are more important than mine. As a result, my needs don't often get met. **Assertiveness** keeps communication open and satisfying while passive or aggressive behaviors make communication unsuccessful. People end up feeling isolated or frustrated and/or misunderstood. For techniques for turning passive or aggressive behavior into assertive behavior see Chapter Four.

Take Aways:

1. Two huge keys for valuable communication are to become aware of your listening blocks and to express yourself assertively.

2. The goals of real listening are to understand, enjoy, learn or help, while pseudo-listening has ulterior motives.

3. In the first key you identify your personal listening blocks and use the tool of "Oh, there it is" to reduce the use of these blocks.

4. The second key of effective communication is to assess your level of assertiveness in order to know yourself better.

5. Passive people value relationships over their other goals. Aggressive people value their personal or professional goals over their relationships. Assertive people weigh their goals and relationships equally.

6. Use the tool of "Can I Move to the Middle?" when you're faced with a difficult situation where you feel you're not being seen or heard. Notice your tendency

to move toward passivity or aggression and see if you can pull yourself toward the middle zone of assertiveness.

CHAPTER THREE

Mastering Your Breath Is the Secret Weapon That Can Change Your Moods

D id you know:

- There are different styles of breathing?
- Your mood impacts your breathing?
- By paying attention to an unconscious pattern and learning to take breaths that work to calm your body

you can both improve your mood and your ability to communicate?

It's simple and true. Feeling anger, sadness or anxiety can produce a certain kind of restricted breathing. The most effective communication happens when you're feeling calm and open. Armed with just a few simple breathing techniques you can change the way you feel and therefore how you interact with others.

Breathing better = Communicating better

Do you know how to take a breath in a way that truly relaxes you?

How many times have you been under stress and reminded yourself that you should probably "just take a breath"? It can be a powerful go-to skill if done correctly. But taking a breath in a way that truly lowers stress is poorly understood and rarely taught. In fact, most often when people take a breath they simply fill their chest with air. But did you know that a chest-only breath won't relax you? We all have our own styles of breathing: some breathe more in our chest, some more in our middles and some in our lower belly. To calm down you need to breathe into either your midsection or belly. This is called diaphragmatic and abdominal breathing.

This chapter will teach you about three major breathing restriction styles that can interfere with full deep breathing. I'll also teach you about the nervous system and breathing to improve communication.

How Do I Breathe?

Take a moment right now and look at yourself taking a breath. You can stand in front of a mirror to see or place your hand on your body to feel where your breath moves.

Now see if you can answer the following questions:

- When I take a breath which part of my body fills up? Is it the upper part of my chest or the lower part near my belly?
- Does my body seem fuller in one place more than another?
- Does my body seem more restricted in one place over another?

If it's hard to tell exactly what's going on in your body, welcome to the club. When I do this exercise in my office most people find it difficult at first because I'm asking them to pay attention to something they haven't paid attention to before, since breathing is mostly automatic. Yet if you become more aware of your breath you can master a breathing style that can greatly affect your emotions and moods. And guess what? Your mood directly impacts the way you communicate.

What does it mean to have "restricted breath"?

Ever have a long stressful day at work but then you get in the car and the drive home is a breeze, the weather is great and your favorite music comes on the radio? Chances are your breathing becomes relaxed and easy and by the time you walk in the door at home you'll greet your family happily. On the other hand, can you call to mind a time when you had a long day at work and then on the drive home you hit traffic, fought bad weather or got pulled over by a policeman for a minor infraction? In this instance you might walk in the door and be grumpy and short when you greet your family. One reason is that most likely when you encountered traffic and got pulled over, you were unconsciously restricting your breath.

How the Breath Reacts Under Threat

Under stress we (often unconsciously) restrict our breath in some manner. Why do we do that? When we perceive any kind of threat we become more alert to assess the danger. For example, what might happen if you heard a loud sudden bang right now? You would likely take in a quick short breath. This is your body automatically preparing for flight or fight in case you're in real danger. In our modern lives, we may feel stress often and therefore we may think that restricted breathing is normal breathing. Because it's something we don't think about, this breathing style can become chronic and unconscious.

Before I introduce my cartoons that illustrate the three styles of breathing restrictions, here's a figure that shows the respiratory organs in a more realistic style. As you know, we need a constant stream of oxygen to stay alive. The respiratory system brings oxygen to the body while also removing carbon dioxide. The three major parts of the respiratory system are the airway, the lungs and the diaphragm.

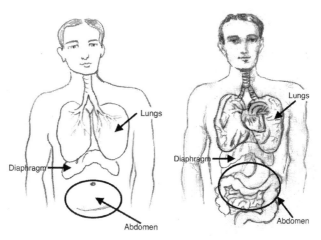

Below the breathing tube are the lungs; the jellyfish-looking organ below the lungs is the diaphragm; and below that is the stomach and intestines which are part of the abdomen. These three—the lungs, the diaphragm and abdomen—will figure into breathing restrictions.

Three Common Styles of Restricted Breath

While there may be many variations of restricted breathing, here are three common styles. Knowing how you feel most of the time will help you uncover your most common breathing style. See if in this next section you can identify being closer to one style than the other.

1. Anxious Breath
2. Collapsed Breath
3. High Energy Breath

When you're trying to uncover which way you might be breathing take a moment to think about how you generally feel. What's your mood most of the time?

1. Anxious Breath

If you tend toward feeling fearful or anxious, your breathing may be shallow and mostly in your chest. If this is your pattern and you need to "take a breath":

➜ DO breathe slowly in your lower belly. This should calm you.

➜ DO NOT breathe quickly and do not breathe only in your chest. This might make you more anxious.

2. <u>Collapsed Breath</u>

If your tendency is to feel sad or blue then you may often be breathing in a shallow manner with a collapsed chest. You may not inhale fully in your chest. If this is your pattern and you want to "take a breath":

➔ DO stretch your back to open your chest. Then take deeper breaths in your chest and diaphragm to feel more energized.

➔ DO NOT curl up into a ball and breathe shallowly or slowly.

3. <u>High Energy Breath</u>

If your tendency is to be high energy and you need to be very active, then you may experience an inflated chest filled with air. If this is your pattern and you want to "take a breath":

➜ DO practice exhaling more fully, expelling all the air from your chest before inhaling. Then breathe in, expanding your abdomen to feel more balanced.

➜ DO NOT take a bigger, chest only inhale.

Breath Techniques

No matter what style of restricted breathing you tend toward, the following two breath techniques can help you. Think about it: by simply breathing in a certain way you can easily de-stress, lessen your anger or anxiety level and buy yourself some time so you can communicate more effectively. By mastering your breath, you'll be able to create an immediate and powerful shift in your mood.

However, your body won't be used to a new way of breathing and may fight the change. It's the same as when you start working on any new healthy habit, for example going to the gym. It might feel uncomfortable or difficult at first but if you keep at it, it becomes easier. Because re-learning a breathing style can be difficult, be sure to be patient with yourself. Use your hands to feel the area, look at your body and practice often.

If you do, you'll be able to quickly and reliably call for a breath shift whenever you're under stress. For instance, when I feel stressed out I tend to tighten my diaphragm. I've learned how to quickly relax my diaphragm by using the following technique.

TOOL: Breathing From Your Diaphragm

Place one hand below your chest with your little finger on your navel as in the diaphragm breath figure. Spread your fingers and press your entire hand firmly on your skin. Your hand is now resting on your diaphragm. Consciously press your hand in as you push your diaphragm out on the next inhalation and breathe in slowly through your nose to the count of four.

1…2…3…4

Pause at the top of the breath. Relax your shoulders and exhale slowly to the count of seven.

1...2...3...4...5...6...7

Take a moment to notice if you have any change in your mood. Then breathe again in the same manner (inhale to the count of four as you push the diaphragm out; exhale slowly to the count of seven and relax). Notice any shifts.

CAUTION: Most people tend to pull up in their chest rather than push out with the diaphragm. Go slowly to attain the effect. You may get dizzy if you're not used to breathing this deeply. Stop and take a break if you feel dizzy.

DIAPHRAGM BREATH FIGURE

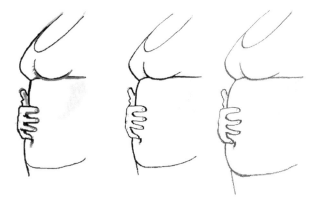

TOOL: Breathing From Your Abdomen

Place one hand firmly on your belly by putting your thumb on your navel and firmly resting the rest of your hand on your belly. Your hand is now resting on your abdomen. Consciously press your hand in as you push your belly out with the next inhalation and breathe in slowly through your nose to the count of four. Pause at the top of the breath. Relax your body and exhale to the count of seven. Take a moment to notice any change in your mood. Repeat this exercise at least twice and breathe again in the same manner (inhale, push belly out; exhale, relax). What did you notice?

CAUTION: Go slowly and concentrate on pushing your abdomen out on the inhalation. Stop if you feel dizzy. Some people find this easier to practice while lying down. That's because your back is relaxed and less likely to compensate for new movements. Once you can achieve these two patterns lying down, do it sitting with your back against a firm chair and then do it standing.

ABDOMEN BREATH FIGURE

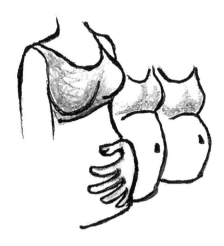

What the Breathing Techniques Can Mean in Your Everyday Life

These two simple techniques can provide an instant shift in your breathing pattern, which will allow you to feel more present and help you to communicate better. This is because as you relax, you feel more centered. When you feel more centered, feelings become clearer and thinking comes back online. Clearer thinking broadens your choices, which can contribute to a more compassionate attitude toward yourself and others.

You may be wondering: Why can't we communicate as well when we're angry, anxious, sad or depressed? Many find it highly frustrating that they can't communicate effectively when they're in agitated states. I mean, after all, isn't that the time we need to communicate the most, when we might need others the most? Let's look to neuroscience for some of the answers.

THE NERVOUS SYSTEM AND BREATH

Why can't I communicate when I'm stressed? This section will answer that by explaining our arousal system and show you how to shift moods in the red, green and blue zones.

On the next page is a chart showing details of the arousal system. The chart is adapted from one created by Ogden, Minton and Pain in 2006 and from Corrigan, Fisher and Nutt in 2010. Faces were added by Vincentia Schroeter in 2015.

High-hyperarousal (SNS) THE RED ZONE
Normal: fight/flight (anger, fear); mobilization.

Under threat: Increased sensations, flooded, emotional reactivity, hypervigilance, intrusive imagery, flashbacks, disorganized cognitive processing, anxiety, impulsivity.

Optimal arousal zone (SES) THE GREEN ZONE
Normal: arousal capacity "window of tolerance"
Ventral vagal (where emotions can be tolerated and information integrated)
Calm, engaged.

Under threat: trouble communicating (move automatically to SNS, if that fails move to PNS).

Low-hypoarousal (PNS) THE BLUE ZONE
Normal: rest, relax, digest, immobilization without fear (safe in arms of another).

Under Threat: Dorsal vagal "immobilization" response, shock, relative absence of sensation; Numbing of emotions, depression, dissociation; disabled cognitive processing, reduced physical movement

AROUSAL CHART

Remember the GREEN, RED and BLUE zones from Chapter One? The chart with the faces has added detail of the arousal zones. It shows the nervous system names and how zones react under normal and threat conditions. The textbox defines the functions of the SNS, SES, and PNS.

SNS=sympathetic nervous system; the part of us ready to fight or flee as a protection.

SES=social engagement system; the part of us that can engage in a calm way.

PNS=parasympathetic nervous system; the part of us that can rest and relax but also freeze and space out if we need that as protection.

Let's take a look at each one of them and how they reflect what's going on in your nervous system. The beauty of speaking in zones is that we can easily identify from our mood when we're in each one. I've found in my work that even children as young as five can relate to moods and label them by zone colors.

Here's an explanation of the ZONES under normal then stress conditions in seeking connection, as well as the normal progression from GREEN to RED to BLUE under stress. I'll add notes on breathing at each arousal level.

The Green Zone (SES)

First, we look for and reach for someone who'll accept and care for us. We use our "social engagement" (SES) system to engage with them. In the green zone we're both calm and can engage well with others. We have both our thinking and open heart available as we engage. We enjoy being both close to others and exploring our world. We feel safe and secure.

NORMAL RANGE: In the GREEN our arousal is optimal. We can tolerate our emotions and integrate information. We can think and feel at the same time.

STRESS RANGE: There's no stress range in the GREEN. As soon as we notice we have trouble communicating we move to the RED to apply energy to get through to others.

BREATH: Our breath is generally relaxed and full. The inhale is relaxed in order to "take in" the world, while the full exhale reflects confidence in "expressing" outwardly in the world.

The Red Zone (SNS)

If that reaching fails, we reach out more vigorously. We more actively assert our needs. A baby may cry or fuss to assert needs and most of us get increasingly anxious and/or angry when not getting our needs met. In the red zone we fight or flee due to the discomfort we feel. We're now using the sympathetic nervous system (SNS).

NORMAL RANGE: The RED zone gives us the energy to work hard at tasks. We're mobilized with more energy for sports, competitions, creativity or other goals. We apply pressure to succeed.

STRESS RANGE: If tension escalates we'll become more aggressive to be heard or withdraw if we feel unheard. We can get hyper, anxious, flooded with sensations or feelings and emotionally reactive. The higher we get in the RED, the less able we are to think clearly.

BREATH: Breath is activated to give us energy as we mobilize for action but under increasing stress can feel pressured and tense.

The Blue Zone (PNS)

If that aggression or withdrawal fails, we give up reaching and withdraw into a depressed, frozen or spaced out place to protect ourselves from the pain. In the blue zone we're now using the parasympathetic nervous system (PNS). The blue zone moves us into a slower, more relaxed state.

NORMAL RANGE: The function of the BLUE zone is for resting and digesting.

STRESS RANGE: The function of the BLUE zone under stress is to immobilize the organism as a response to feeling defeated or trapped. We often get immobilized in conversations when we're shocked or deeply hurt. As a response we numb our emotions and get still, leading to depression or dissociation. It's nearly impossible to find words to communicate clearly from this state.

BREATH: Breath can be slow and relaxed (while resting or digesting) but under stress gets restricted and very shallow. This shallow breath is dangerous for the health of the human heart if we stay in that state too long.

RED ZONE

DOWN REGULATING

GREEN ZONE

How to Shift From Red to Green

Although these shifts from one state to another are automatic, we can change them with awareness. A person who wants to communicate clearly will want to come from the green zone where communication is best. That's where we're feeling safe. When we feel safe we can easily access both our feelings and our thoughts. What can we do if we're not in the calm engaged state and we need to communicate? Let's say we're in the RED and need to be in the GREEN! How can we get there?

1. Become aware. Anger is too high when we feel frustration, rage or an impulse toward harsh language or violence. You may feel the heat of anger in your body. Maybe your fists ball up or your jaw tightens. You might notice that you feel a mix of anger and anxiety. You may feel compelled to strike out. This means your heat is rising up in the RED ZONE. Or you may feel an

impulse to flee and feel your legs wanting to run away. This is also a RED ZONE reaction.

2. Learn how to "down regulate". To be able to communicate with grounded compassion when you're too high in the RED ZONE is pretty much impossible. You'll need to "**down regulate**" (or come down from the anger or fear) by breathing deeply and slowly until the anger cools and fear calms before choosing your next words. Think of it as going from too hot, like boiling water to cool, like after blowing on a hot drink for a while. Once you feel cooler, calmer and kinder, find the words and then communicate.

<u>Example: Brandy's Story - Shifting from Red to Green</u>
Brandy tells her co-worker, Sally, about a fight with her husband.

Brandy: "When I get mad I stay mad at him for a long time." (RED)

Sally: "I get it. So what helps you feel less mad?"

Brandy: "I like to go in my room, close the door and lie on my bed."

Sally: "Then what happens?"

Brandy: "I think he hates me, that everybody hates me. I get scared, then I feel lonely and sometimes I cry for a while."

Sally: "How long do you cry?"

Brandy: "Until I feel all cried out, I guess. Then I come down and I can talk to him about what happened." (back to GREEN)

NOTE: Had Brandy not cried to release the hurt she may have needed outside help to move out of the RED ZONE. Crying (like laughing) loosens the diaphragm and causes deeper breathing. Once she released her tears Brandy's breath was deeper and more relaxed. This allowed her to feel renewed hope as she naturally moved back to the GREEN ZONE, which allowed her to be able to reconnect with her husband.

Shifting From the Blue to the Green Zone

It's difficult to communicate well in the BLUE ZONE because we're far away from feeling like connecting to others, lost in our dark cave of protection. Have you ever felt that way?

For example, have you ever experienced a time when someone you love has hurt or betrayed you in a big way? You feel shocked. You pull in to yourself and may feel disorganized. Your whole sense of what was normal can change instantly. It's so difficult to tolerate this new reality that it can feel like a small death. You don't want to move your body as a heavy stillness overtakes you and your brain becomes foggy. You don't feel like yourself.

Most of us have had times like that. This is the BLUE ZONE pulling us in for self-protection against (what may feel like to the body) annihilation. Some people feel shame for not being able to move out from this place but it's important to understand that our nervous system is doing this to make us feel safe. Although we may need to go to the BLUE ZONE at times, if you stay there a long time it can be dangerous to the body because our stress levels remain very high and it can mess with our mental stability and heart. It's important to know ways to get out.

In the BLUE ZONE we shut down and breathe in a shallow manner like when we're sick. When you have the flu your energy is low and it feels like your world shrinks. You're less active or mobile. If we're in the BLUE and want to get back to the GREEN how can we get there? We need to "**up-regulate**" (find a way to rise up from a still place). We need to get mobilized again.

GREEN ZONE

UP REGULATING

BLUE ZONE

How to Shift From the BLUE Back to the GREEN ZONE

1. Become aware of your state. Notice in your body where you feel closed off and pulled in. This is where breathing can act as a crucial link.
2. Learn how to "up regulate." Breathe deeply both inhaling and exhaling fully to energize the body and make it more mobile. This can help us to feel more grounded, which will move us back to the GREEN ZONE. Anything that brings energy to the body, such as physical exercise, will also help us go toward the GREEN.

I invite you to try these exercises and be patient with yourself. It takes a while to master up and down regulating. However, as soon as you bring awareness to being in the red or the blue zone and want to down regulate from the red or up regulate from the blue, that neuropathway will get stronger and it will move faster each time. The reward is to be able to access the desirable green zone quickly to feel safer and ultimately to improve communication.

Take Aways:

1. Three major breathing restriction patterns interfere with full deep breathing. They are anxious, collapsed and high energy breathing styles.

2. Taking a diaphragmatic breath can reduce tension and relax the body.

3. Taking an abdominal breath can reduce tension and relax the body.

4. The RED and BLUE zones have both normal and stress functions.

5. By getting to the SES (social engagement system) in the GREEN zone we feel biologically safest and can best communicate thoughts and feelings.

6. Breathing techniques can help move a person down (down regulating) from high states of anger or anxiety in the RED zone.

7. Breathing techniques can help mobilize or move a person up out of (up regulate) depressive or low states in the BLUE zone.

CHAPTER FOUR

Discover the Tricks to Becoming More Assertive

When assessing your personality style it's pretty normal to find yourself either leaning more towards passivity or aggression. As discussed in Chapter Two, if people see you as too aggressive, bossy or pushy, you may turn people off. They may retreat from you, which is not what you want. If people see you as being too shy or passive you may find that you're passed over without being noticed, which is also not what you want.

So what do most people want? They want to be taken seriously, to be heard and to be understood. The best way to have that happen is to move toward a more assertive communication style.

If you lean toward passivity you can learn "Standing Up" techniques to help you speak up and practice becoming more assertive. If you lean toward aggression I can teach you several practical and dynamic "Standing Down" tools so you can practice being more assertive and less aggressive. I'll show you that your brain on rage has a predictable and automatic behavior pattern. I'll also help you identify your anger triggers and then provide two techniques to contain your aggression in case of a flare-up. Finally, I'll teach you how to use the stress scale to measure your "before and after" states of anger, which can help you figure out what techniques work best for you.

Tackling Passivity: Standing Up, Talking Straight

How can you learn to stand up for yourself in everyday situations? The answer is quite simple: you need support. That support can come from two places.

Yourself → Internal Support
Others → External Support

How to Support Yourself: Internal Support

When you tend toward passivity your natural protective urge is to shrink and hide away rather than to stand up for yourself. Standing up feels risky and tough to do. In order to strengthen the ability to stand up for yourself it helps to feel strong on the inside. Internal support offers a way to feel more confident and powerful on a body level and in your mind. The following technique helps you feel stronger in your body while calling on a positive view to assert yourself. Even if you didn't receive much positive support as a child and you have some critical voices inside, you can add an encouraging voice as a first step in building an internal support system now. Here are the steps.

SELF TALK → MOVE → BODY POSTURE → PRACTICE → PRAISE

SELF TALK

Talk to your scared or reluctant self as if you were an encouraging parent. For example, "You can do it! I'll be right here beside you."

MOVE

Get out and move your body (taking into consideration any physical limitations). A muscle strengthening physical regimen such as a simple workout can help you to feel physically stronger, which can spread to a general feeling of overall strength and added confidence.

BODY POSTURE

It may sound overly simple but learning how to place your body in the right positions can increase your sense of internal strength and help you be more assertive. Place your body in the following stance and practice what you'll say to stand up for yourself (what they did, how you feel and what you want). When you're about to stand up to someone move your body in the following ways before you speak up:

- Stand up straight or sit up straight.
- Lean forward.
- Tip your head down slightly while looking the other person in the eye.

PRACTICE

Pick a situation and practice asserting your need **one time this week** (e.g. return rotten food to the grocery store, speak up if someone cuts in line ahead of you or decline an offer to socialize if you don't want to be with that person or go to that event). Just as lifting weights builds arm muscles, practicing being assertive will build and strengthen the brain pathway for more assertive behavior in the future!

PRAISE

Pat yourself on the back. Praise yourself for any successes no matter how small to encourage yourself to keep up the good work. This will help you practice assertive behaviors more often in the future.

How to Gain Support from Others: External Support

Getting external support means enlisting and receiving the help of others. The assistance of others can help you feel more grounded so you have a stronger sense of self-acceptance. This can fuel your ability to be assertive in appropriate ways. To enlist help, confide in a trusted friend or therapist. Share with them your desire to become more assertive. Imagine their support as a hand on your back when you go to assert your needs.

Tackling Aggression: Standing Down, Talking Clearly

If you're on the other end of the spectrum and you tend toward being too aggressive, you may not know how to **calmly** assert your needs. When in a troubling situation you might feel a sense of impatience, experience a feeling of losing control and then find that you've gone overboard. If you find yourself in this arena please don't feel bad about it or beat yourself up. We're often not taught in school (and often not taught at home) how to handle anger in healthy ways. So just think of it as gaining some useful insight and assistance for times when you face an angry moment, a flare-up or a flash of anger.

If you tend to be aggressive and want to be assertive it's important to decode how your brain is actually working when you're flooded with these feelings. You'll be learning how to cool down to be able to communicate in a calmer yet still assertive manner. Let's start by…

Understanding the Brain on Rage

Ever wonder what's happening inside your brain when you face that moment of anger? It's helpful to take a quick peek inside.

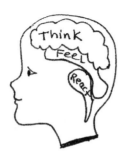

Aggressive acts can happen so fast because we can move from feeling in control to feeling out of control very quickly. To put it simply, when we're flooded with angry feelings our body interprets them as a threat. When we feel threatened our body is actually preparing for battle. It wants to keep us safe from real (or imagined) danger. All our senses go automatically into fight or flight mode. In other words, when that flash of anger wells up inside you, your body is reacting from a primal place. And there's a reason this primal reaction exists. Without this instinct our ancestors wouldn't have survived. They were faced with real and present dangers and they needed to immediately move into either fight or flight, or else they would have perished. Appreciating that our body reaction is just part of our biology can help reduce guilt as we work to manage our anger.

Although our brains will still automatically move into fight or flight mode, the actual danger is often not as serious as facing a life or death situation. But the brain may not understand that. When we feel flooded with upsetting feelings our anger can be blinding and then we feel a sense of desperation or feeling trapped, both of which can lead to overreacting.

Imagine the common scenario of being in an overcrowded public parking lot. You have 10 minutes to get to an important business meeting and there are simply no parking spots. Finally, you see a car leaving and you arrive first in line to move into that spot. Only as soon as the car vacates the spot, another car zooms in and steals your spot. You might feel your body flooded with angry and upsetting feelings. Thinking that this person just robbed you of being on time to your meeting, your sense of desperation may increase and you may find yourself experiencing red-hot rage.

Looking objectively at the situation: Is it life or death? No.

Looking at what's going on inside your brain: Can it activate the life or death, fight or flight response? Yes, it can.

What is Rage?

Rage is like hot lava scorching the mountain and flooding the land to make it uninhabitable for people. People are burned and damaged by the rage of others.

Think of a thermometer that's designed to measure temperature. When the weather is hot the thermometer rises. When we flare in anger our temperature rises and we "flip our lid." In a way that's what happens in the brain. Our lid (or top of the brain) is the thinking part called the neo-cortex. When the brain pops open its top (boils over in rage) thinking is gone and we're left with the more primitive limbic (emotional) and reptilian (fight/flight/freeze) parts of the brain.

All the learned good communication skills go out the window as the neo-cortex (thinking) part of the brain melts in the fire of rage. How can we cool the fire in the moment? To become more assertive and less aggressive, you can rein in rage by pulling back, slowing down and speaking up in a more contained way. Let's look at two examples.

Exploring Your Personal Anger Triggers

We all have issues that irritate us or try our patience. We might find that we have less patience than others in certain situations due to past experiences, which often relate to an old emotional wound. It's valuable for you to know these triggers and to humbly respect their power to derail your ability to act rationally at times. For example, let's say a teacher bullied you in the classroom. If you encounter a situation where you see a child getting pushed around by a teacher you may get triggered and more easily lose your temper than someone who hadn't had that personal experience as a child. Completing the few sentences below will help you get in touch with what pushes your buttons.

Complete these sentences:

What makes me really angry?
   A. When people_____
   B. When I_____
   C. When the world_____
   D. When (name of person/group_____ is _____

Example:

What makes me really angry?
A. When adults bully kids.
B. When I feel like I'm not being heard or understood.
C. When the world doesn't take into account how the little guy feels.
D. When my daughter's teacher is rude to my daughter and makes her feel like she doesn't matter.

Four Tools to Contain Aggression: Standing Down

I'm going to teach you four dynamic tools to help you better understand your behavior, relax yourself and calm your overactive brain. The first technique is the "7-Step Cool Down" and the second is "Name It to Tame It." The third, "3 Fast Ways to Avoid a Fight" helps when the situation has escalated and you want to avoid a big confrontation. The final tool is "What Am I Thinking?" and can help you better understand what thoughts are going on inside your head when you're in a state of high stress. We'll start with a case example to show the value of the "7-Step Cool Down" method.

Scott's Story: The 7-Step Cool Down

Scott and Jenny were seeing me because they wanted to work on what they called "poor communication" in their marriage. Jenny complained that Scott got angry a lot and had trouble sharing his thoughts with her in a calm manner. On our third session Scott became heated and agitated and I was able to observe the behavior Jenny had spoken about. Jenny asked him why he was so mad about their finances. Scott leaned forward and was fuming with so much anger that he simply couldn't think how to communicate without saying something attacking that might start a fight. I guided him to take a moment, stop talking, press his feet into the floor, lean his back into the sofa, look at and breathe into his lower abdomen and take four slow breaths. This simple technique contained his anger, grounded his body, calmed him down and allowed him to get his thinking back online. After a minute or so Scott was able to tell Jenny his feelings in a calmer manner.

7-Step Cool Down

Here are 7 easy-to-follow steps that can help you to contain your aggression in an anger flare-up moment.

1. Stop talking and get quiet.
2. Press your feet into the floor.
3. Lean your back firmly into the chair.
4. Look at your stomach and take four slow breaths into your belly.
5. Check to see if you feel more kind-hearted. If so then say to your partner, "I appreciate that you're trying to communicate with me right now."
6. If you don't feel kind-heartedness return, continue deep breathing or ask to continue the conversation when you're less angry.
7. Consider a time-out: Get up and leave after promising to return to discuss the issues in 30 or 60 minutes or whenever you've cooled down. Use self-compassion while on your timeout. (Self-compassion here would be to remind yourself that this is how we're all wired: to flare into anger when overstressed. This is just our

biology. To reverse it we just need this time-out break.) Review the series of events in your head that led to your time-out.

If you're angry you may need to reach out to someone to validate what you're experiencing by asking them to listen to your story. If you're so angry that you can't talk and listen clearly, you may need some physical comfort to calm down. Since your feelings are strong in rage, take a few breaths to assess what kind of outside (if any) support you need.

If someone else is in a rage you can be his or her external resource. A quick and easy technique to act as a resource for someone in a state of rage is the "Name It to Tame It" technique. This technique comes from *The Whole Brain Child* by Dan Siegel and Tina Bryson.

Name It to Tame It

When someone is in a rage they may be trapped in the part of the brain that houses the more primitive emotional defense system or what can be called their "downstairs" brain. The upset person in the rage is the speaker. The technique involves listening to their story and their feelings and repeating what you heard back to them in a calm and understanding tone. Repeating the story activates the "upstairs" (thinking) brain of the speaker. Then a shift can happen. Being seen and feeling heard is soothing and helps the person move their brain toward critical thinking and processing. Siegel and Bryson explain that when someone is so upset that they can't access the "upstairs" brain on their own, it's a sign of a level of disorganization that needs nurturing and comfort from an external source. Once comforted by someone else, the person is usually better able to organize his or her own thoughts and feelings.

Renee and Laura: An Example of "Name It to Tame It"

A few years ago, Renee, a combative seven-year old girl and her mother Laura came to see me for some help. Renee was active in the office circling around the furniture and jumping on the mat. Laura told her to stop jumping on the mat. Renee became furious and barked loudly at her mother. Laura looked at me as if to ask how to handle all the anger that was being thrown her way.

I went to Renee's side and said in an understanding tone, "You were having fun jumping, then your mother told you to stop jumping, then you looked frustrated, then you got mad and then you yelled at her. Is that what happened?"

Having felt seen and understood Renee stopped being angry. Her mother was shocked to see how "Name It to Tame It" (repeating the sequence of events including the feelings) calmed Renee down almost immediately.

Why this technique works so well:

When you engage the upset or angry person in reviewing the entire series of events, he or she feels seen and heard. This helps the brain move away from primitive reactivity and toward critical thinking and processing.

3 Fast Ways to Avoid a Fight

Use "3 Fast Ways to Avoid a Fight" to help you walk away from the kind of situation that could lead to a fight. First, let's talk about what our body goes through quickly and automatically. When we're ready to fight, the big muscles in the arms and legs engorge with energy. Anger rides up the back, then over the head, and then anger comes through the eyes, voice and the arms, which prepare the body to strike. This is our biology kicking in and preparing the body to challenge and confront our opponent. So if the body can reverse that movement we can cool down and buy time to re-think our aggressive impulses.

1. Walking away from the source of distress will usually help you cool down.

2. Another technique is to take the energy that you may feel wanting to rise up and use gravity to move it down in the opposite direction. How to do this: While standing bend and straighten your knees 10 times while breathing slowly. Steady your body by holding a hand on a wall or by not bending as deeply if it affects your balance. Each time you bend your knees count to four before rising again. After these 10 slow knee bends assess your anger level. (CAUTION: Only do this body movement if it's safe for you. Just bend and stretch in ways you can manage easily.)

3. If you still feel too much anger to think and communicate clearly, you may need to discharge your anger (or the feelings underlying it like fear or hurt). Get away from those you're angry at. Grab a pillow, bury your face in it and scream into the pillow. Vocalize your stress, anger and/or fear as those feelings arise. If your feelings turn into hurt, discharge your hurt through

crying into the pillow. Check in again to see if you've lowered your high anger charge by releasing these feelings.

You can also consult a psychotherapist trained to support expressive movements. Bioenergetic therapists are trained in psychology but also use somatic exercises to help with containment or expression of emotions. The Bioenergetic therapist is trained to read and understand tension patterns in your body related to emotional issues and like other therapists s/he becomes a safe sounding board to help you deal with your problems.

Using the Stress Scale

This technique is easy and fast. When you find yourself in a negative or angry space take a moment to write down the cause of the anger, any negative thoughts that are floating around your brain and your current anger level. Measure your current anger level using the 0-5 stress scale. Next, do an exercise from this chapter such as walking away, breathing slowly or bending your knees 10 times with the breathing. Next, pay attention to that negative thought and see if you can form a more reasonable thought. Finally, measure your anger level on the stress scale again.

-5

-4

-3

-2

-1

-0

(5) **Highest, Most Intense Stress** → overwhelmed; extreme thoughts related to the defense of fight/flight.

(4) **High Stress** → ruffled but feel some control; may not be clear on why.

(3) **Middling Stress** → stressed and may need to notice why; do emotional housekeeping; bring compassion, acceptance and non-judgment to focus on and understand your emotional state.

(2) **Low-Middle Stress** → feel some stress but generally able to identify feeling and re-ground or re-center self.

(1) **Low Stress** → notice mild stress but feel accepting and flexible in ability to manage and respond.

What Am I Thinking?

A Written Exercise to Help Manage Anger

A. Cause of anger: _____

B. Negative thought /emotion: _____

C. Anger level (0=low, 5=high):_____

D. Body calming exercise: ____(do the physical exercise)

E. Reasonable thought: _____

F. Anger level (0=low, 5=high): _____

Example for this Exercise:

A. Cause of anger: When driver cuts me off.
B. Negative thought: He did it on purpose; emotion: annoyance.
C. Current anger level on 0-5: 4-5.
D. Body technique: Breathe slowly two times.
E. Re-assess unreasonable thought: "He did it on purpose to mess with me." Consider reasonable thought: "He was distracted, not paying attention but he wasn't out to get me."
F. Anger level on stress scale: 2-3.

There will be times when you've practiced a few techniques but felt you were still struggling. Here are a few final tips and tools to help get you through a rough moment.

Other Ideas for Cooling Down if Still Not Calm

Put your hand on your belly and take three very slow breaths. With your hand firmly on your belly place your thumb on your navel. Your hand is now resting on your abdomen (see abdomen breath figure in Chapter Three). Consciously press your hand in as you push your belly out with the next inhalation and breathe in slowly through your nose to the count of four. Pause at the top of the breath. Relax your body and exhale to the count of seven. Take a moment to notice any change in your mood. Think of yourself and the other person you're angry at. Be non-judgmental while breathing in compassion for yourself and for them. Next, use the positive affirmation, "I deserve compassion. S/he deserves compassion." Shrug your shoulders as if you were "shrugging it off." Minimize any actions that may cause harm or escalate conflict. (Stay away from doing anything like raising your voice, making a challenge or physically moving toward the person you're angry at.) Say to yourself, "This too shall pass" and then walk away and distract yourself. Do your best to redirect your energy somewhere else like listening to music or remembering a positive story or funny joke. Distraction is a helpful tool in a pinch. As time passes without focusing on your anger, the anger often cools down. Remember that the goal of these exercises is to avoid overreacting in an aggressive way. Once you "stand down" and are calmer your brain will naturally return to a place where you can act in a way you'll feel better about later. This allows you to be less aggressive yet more assertive by standing up for yourself, while thoughtfully considering the other person. From this place your needs are more likely to be met.

Which Tool is Best For Me?

In this chapter I've introduced you to a number of techniques for calming down. If you're wondering which ones will be the most effective for you, check the stress scale. The next time you're feeling overheated take a look at that (0-5) scale and pick the number you identify with at that moment. Then do one of the techniques. After completing the technique take a look at the stress scale once more. How far down the scale did you travel by using that technique? Measuring your "before and after" states of anger is a quick and easy way to pinpoint which techniques work best for you.

Take Aways:

1. When assessing your personality style, it's normal to find yourself leaning either towards passivity or aggression.

2. If you lean toward passivity you can learn techniques to speak up and practice becoming more assertive.

3. If you lean toward aggression you now know that the brain on rage has a predictable and automatic behavior pattern.

4. A 7-point technique for containing aggression can help you in the moment of any flare-up and a 3-step technique can help the body to stand down.

5. Exploring your anger triggers can help you to manage your flare-ups.

6. Using the stress scale to measure your "before and after" states of anger can help you figure out which techniques work best for you.

CHAPTER FIVE

Train Your Brain to Become the Best Listener Ever

Sally: "But I AM listening to you!"
Ted: "No, you aren't!"

*H**ave you ever felt like Sally?* You know, when you were sure you were listening to someone talking and found it frustrating that the other person complained that they weren't being heard? *Have you ever felt like Ted?* Where you felt as if you were speaking but not truly being heard even though you were doing your best to communicate?

If two people are doing their best and both have a valid point of view, who's the culprit here? The answer is that poor listening skills may be causing the problem.

In Chapter Two, I asked you to assess your listening skills by deciding which listening blocks you may unknowingly be using. Remember we all use blocks at times especially when we're distracted or tired. The goal in this chapter is to learn how to apply the solution: Active listening skills. I'll be teaching you:

- How to practice active listening (paraphrase, clarify, give feedback).
- How to get fast communication results from whole brain listening.
- How the LOWER brain goes into survival mode under severe stress.
- The 6 tools for accessing the UPPER (thinking) brain for listening when the LOWER (emotional) brain is overwhelmed.
- How to train your brain in new and different ways when it has previously been trained to travel down old worrisome roads.

The 6 Magic Listening Skills

Now that you've identified at least a few of your listening blocks from your assessment in Chapter Two, take a moment to think of a time when you felt as if someone truly listened to you. How did you feel? What did the person say or do? Chances are that within that experience lie the three components that identify ACTIVE listening.

When someone practices active listening, others feel heard. Active listening means to:

1. **Listen with full attention** (the desire to hear and understand).
2. **Listen for feelings as well as content** (use empathy to put yourself in their shoes).
3. **Actively acknowledge what you've heard** (both the content and feelings).

Some people struggle trying to figure out how to express number three, actively acknowledging what they heard. Here are some specific ways you can actively acknowledge what the speaker just said to you:

4. **Paraphrase → say in your own words what you heard.**
5. **Clarify → if you're not sure, ask questions to get clear on the speaker's meaning.**
6. **Give feedback which has three parts:**
   - Immediate: respond soon without delay.
   - Honest: your true reaction, revealing your feelings.
   - Supportive: state your honest reaction in a kind way.

An Example of Active Listening: Calling Mom

Ken hated calling his mother. But feeling obliged he would reluctantly make the weekly call. He dreaded hearing her voice and found he would get anxious and bored as she spoke about her weekly experiences. Ken came to me expressing that he wished there was a way for him to enjoy the weekly ritual a bit more. I presented him with the listening blocks.

Here's a reminder of the 12 **LISTENING BLOCKS:**

1. Comparing (deciding who is smarter, more competent, more popular, etc.)
2. Mind Reading (not paying attention to words and thinking you can read people without having to listen to them)
3. Rehearsing (looking interested but really preparing what you want to say)

4. Filtering (listening for some things and not others, e.g. are they angry at me?)
5. Judging (either pre-judging the speaker or what they say and attaching a negative label which makes you stop listening before you have heard them out)
6. Dreaming (paying attention to only a fraction as your mind wanders elsewhere)
7. Identifying (you identify and can't wait to tell your similar story)
8. Advising (jumping in with unsolicited advice; wanting to fix the problem)
9. Sparring (listening long enough to disagree then assert your opinion; includes sarcasm and put-downs; argue and debate)
10. Being Right (proving you're right including lying, shouting, twisting facts, changing the subject, making excuses and accusing)
11. Derailing (changing the subject or making a joke whenever you're bored or uncomfortable with the conversation)
12. Placating (concerned with being nice, agreeable or liked so you don't really listen and you agree with everything being said)

Ken looked them over and then shared his realizations that he used dreaming, placating and filtering with his mother to "get through the calls." I asked him to practice active listening for their next phone call.

After calling his mom and employing active listening, Ken shared that he felt surprised at the change. He hadn't prejudged what his mother was going to say. He paid attention whenever he found his mind wandering (dreaming). He decided to just be on the phone with his mom and allow the conversation to unfold naturally. Ken shared that for the first time in years he really enjoyed their conversation. He felt he got to know and appreciate his mom in a new way and reported that over the next few weeks their closeness had deepened.

How did Ken succeed so well? He practiced active listening by starting with an open and receptive stance (rather than his usual pre-judging), returning to his breath and paying attention (when he found himself daydreaming), paraphrasing what his mother said (including her feelings) and being supportive. As an unexpected bonus this brought him joy and made him feel closer to his mother.

A Simple and Powerful Listening Practice

Identify someone in your life with whom you might employ a listening block from time to time. Be aware of your listening block before you engage with that person. The next time you talk to him or her use the active listening skills. Listen openly and respond (paraphrase, clarify, give feedback). See what a difference it might make in your relationship!

Whole Brain Listening: Help for When You Can't Listen

While the brain has many complex and interacting parts I'll simplify them by referring to the LOWER and UPPER parts. The LOWER (limbic) part registers most of our sensory and emotional experiences. Those experiences travel to the UPPER (neo-cortex) part, which is where we make meaning of what we experience. "Whole brain" listening refers to bringing together the UPPER (thinking) and LOWER (emotional) parts of the brain in service of listening.

If while listening we hear something disturbing (like when we're being blamed) we may feel threatened and go into a defensive mode, which can cause us to block any further listening. Here's an example where we can get hijacked by the emotional reactivity of the lower part of the brain.

Imagine you're a parent being confronted by your teenager who's mad at you for picking him up late from school.

He says, "I can't believe you're picking me up late again. You screwed this up like you do every time. I hate you."

It's normal to feel angry and/or hurt by these accusations.

Next, your feeling of anger creates an impulse to fight. The last thing you want is to listen further as most likely you now feel wounded.

Let's say the other kids taunted your son while he waited for you. And he'll now be late for sports practice which will embarrass him further. (You don't know this because having been yelled at you have no patience left to listen to the embarrassment under his anger.)

You see something in his eyes, some sort of sadness and there's a part of you that wants to talk it through, to listen to what's happened. But instead you find yourself shouting, "How dare you talk to me like that. You could have texted me. It's your fault for always depending on me for a ride."

Now you're both fuming silently.

At the moment it might have felt good to defend yourself. But at what cost?

Later you may feel bad but the damage is done.

This brings me to our next question:

Why can't we still listen, especially if some part of us really wants to? Here's how it works. If our emotional brain gets so full of feelings (feeling blamed, threatened, ashamed, sad, angry, hurt or scared) that we can't manage them, we feel overwhelmed. It's almost like there's no room left to listen. The emotional brain sounds the alarm and the thinking brain shrinks back and gets out of the way. The stress hormones kick into gear like fireman with hoses of adrenalin to help get us to safety. Feeling threatened makes the brain act like we're walking on a tightrope over a tank of sharks.

As you're walking you most likely won't be able to think of anything but successfully getting to the other side. This leaves no space to consider the other person's perspective, point of view or emotional state.

So in the previous example, you love your son, you know he gets stressed when he has to wait for you to pick him up and you're late. But once he attacked you, your need to defend yourself hijacked your openness to his perspective.

That's why it's so hard to listen during conflict as our poor bodies are just reacting naturally to threat. What can we do under these conditions?

Solving the Problem

How can we create the space to be open to the other person when we're overwhelmed with feelings? The solution is to restore the shrinking upper brain and soothe the overwhelmed lower brain so we can listen with the whole brain.

How To Get The Thinking Brain Up Off The Mat

"I Am Not Listening To You Anymore."

As I've just discussed, it's pretty normal to get flooded with feelings and to stop listening during a triggering conversation. How exactly can the upper part of the brain get back up and help the lower part, when the lower threatens to take over and we can't even listen anymore?

The upper brain is standing back and observing the back and forth dialogue between us and the other person. It's the part of us that knows what we should do. It knows our values and wishes to help us behave sensibly and appropriately. But when we're walking that tightrope over the shark tank we can't hear that tiny "should" voice. It's too far away to have any power.

In order to get the help of the upper brain we have to know how to access it.

When under low stress → both parts of the brain interact easily and smoothly with messages flowing back and forth.

Yet under high stress → the lower brain gets flooded with too much feeling and the upper brain gets drowned out. It's like a tsunami that roars to shore destroying all in its wake. When the emotional brain dominates, the thinking brain has no power.

It's only in calming the lower brain that the upper brain can regain power. How do you get it back online when the lower brain bursts through the dam? Here are some tools that help create the necessary calmness to reactivate the thinking brain.

IMPORTANT NOTE:
CALMNESS IS ESSENTIAL FOR THE THINKING BRAIN TO GET BACK ONLINE.

6 Tools to Calm the Emotional Brain

All these strategies involve helping to calm you down so you can be more present and communicate more effectively.

1. **Put yourself aside.** Tell yourself, "I just need to put myself aside for a moment and pay attention to what the other person is saying." Then take a deep breath (or a few) until you notice yourself becoming calmer.
2. **Search for empathy.** Everyone deserves respect. Remind yourself to listen because the other person wants to express something that's important to him or her.
3. **Be here and now.** "Orienting" is a technique to calm the nervous system when you perceive you're in danger. Look around and assess if you are in real danger. (Look for actual "sharks".) If not, do the following exercise. Orient to the here and now by naming (to yourself) all the colors in the room you're in. Breathe slowly as you do this. Once you feel calmer, sit in a relaxed and open posture with an attitude of receptivity to the speaker.

4. **Utilize mirroring.** Mirroring means to repeat or paraphrase what the speaker just said. If you do this before responding, it slows things down and can help calm you, which buys you time to think more clearly. This is a fantastic trick to utilize. It re-directs your still-stressed-out-system to the task of repeating. Just the act of repeating can be calming.

5. **Go back and forth.** Another technique is "titration." This means going back and forth. First, pay attention to comforting yourself, then switch and pay attention to the speaker. Think of a time in your past when communicating was highly stressful. You likely had trouble thinking. That's why some people stutter or have difficulty finding words in high stress conflicts. Titration, or going back and forth, is useful in high stress situations. For example, if you feel too defensive to think, find some nearby object to use as a buffer for protection. For example, grab and hold a pillow to your chest. Next, drop your head for a few slow breaths. Raise your head and see if you feel calmer and alert to the current situation and able to hear better. In titration you go back and forth from the more closed (head down) posture, which should make you feel some protection and more safety, to the open (head lifted) receptive posture.

6. **Use strategy words or actions.** You can also create your own strategy using words or phrases. Use words such as "peace," "love," "confidence," "strength" or "calm." Think of words describing your positive qualities. Recall helpful sayings (such as my mother's favorite, "This too shall pass"). Use actions such as pressing

your feet into the floor that can calm your body so your thinking brain can emerge and help you to listen more receptively.

I'd like to revisit the earlier example of being a mother about to blow up at her son. Using your new tools you could take a breath slowly with an intention to put yourself aside (1) and listen. Next, think about your son and how he deserves empathy (2). Press your hands against the steering wheel to orient to the here and now (3). Paraphrase what you heard: "You're angry because I picked you up late" (4). Go back and forth between breathing and pressing your hands on the wheel and listening (5). Think of the word "love" and touch your heart as you recall your son laughing and delighting you when he was a baby (6).

Pay attention to see if your body calms. Also, if you did blow up, once you feel calmer, then apologize to your son. Children are usually eager to repair a rift.

How to Get the LOWER Brain on a New Road
Trauma and the Brain

Ever wonder why you might tend to over react when your right brain gets flooded with feelings?

Sometimes we can get flooded with feelings. We may act impulsively, go into crying jags and rages or shrink in fear. In these cases, we've often triggered a reaction from an old trauma or wound. Past emotional wounds create a neural network in the brain, a new road created by the trauma. The next time something similar happens, even if it's not as bad as the first incident, your brain goes down that road expecting the bad outcome just like the first time. Animals react this way too. For example, if his previous owner beat your new dog and you raise your hand to pet him, he may flinch or get aggressive as he expects to be beaten again. Your hand above his head is the trigger that gets him going down the old road.

For our purpose, we'll look at old patterns that interfere with good communication. We can get sucked into a patterned response based on the past, which is like riding a sled down the same mountain path. You create grooves on the first ride.

The second time you climb back to the top of the mountain, the sled is likely to follow the grooves made by the first time you sledded down. These grooves are like the ones created by past habits. We're all trained to have certain reactions. Understanding our past can help us feel compassion toward ourselves and others, since we all have old wounds that might pop up and retrigger us from time to time. Here's a story to show how a childhood wound becomes activated in the present.

Anne's Story

Her mother criticized Anne a lot as a child. She would often have to sit at the kitchen table and silently endure a tirade of criticism while her mother paced back and forth. Anne recently had a job evaluation with her boss. After commenting on her positive qualities, her boss began to tell her of some minor areas that needed improvement. He paced a bit as he spoke. (This pacing reminded Anne of her mother's pacing and was the cue for Anne's reaction.)

Anne started to feel anxiety and anger. She tightened her jaw, shrank in the chair and longed to run away. She pretended to listen politely but in truth she wasn't hearing anything her boss was saying. Anne's body was tightening in the same way it did when she was a child. She was also flooded with the same fear, anger and shame she experienced in the past. This was Anne reacting today like she did when she was a child.

At a certain point in the interaction, Anne stopped listening. Why is that?

Past Trauma Interferes with Listening

When listening, our emotional brains may go into a defensive reaction toward the speaker and off we soar as our sled flies down the familiar path of almost reliving previous a painful experience. The speaker may not intend to take us there. In fact, we may have started on a neutral new path but something familiar in the speaker's words or actions made us join the old path. In our minds, we're sure the path will end the same way as it always had.

These old neural networks can be seen in brain images. The more the old road is used the sturdier it gets. To create a new path is difficult and takes concentrated effort. Most of us, even if we're pretty resilient, have at least one big fear that's due to an earlier familiar wound.

Some common fears are that we'll be criticized, humiliated, controlled, disrespected, exploited, rejected or abandoned. We're sure this is how the ride will end because that's all we know. We may not have any other "template" in our brain that would allow us the flexibility to travel down a new path.

In Anne's case, the criticism was the trigger and she was off and sledding down her old familiar path. She abandoned the speaker who may have been sailing down a far different road. But just by being triggered, Anne was miles away from the conversation that took place in the present. In the following story, the husband is triggered by his wife's critical remark. I counseled them in communication skills.

Mary and John's Story

Mary and John are married. Mary asks John if he can help with their clogged kitchen sink but at that moment John said he was busy completing his work. Angrily, Mary says to her husband, "You're useless; you never help me with anything. Sometimes I wonder if I would be better off without you."

Here's what happens to John. He feels threatened by that remark. It's received like a blow to his body. He shrinks in fear, worried that it might spell the end of his marriage to Mary. John quickly sails down the road remembering how he felt when his father called him useless as a child.

As the listener, John is triggered by fear of rejection and goes sledding down his old familiar path. Now he's walking that tightrope over the sharks (originally father's ability to eviscerate him). For self-preservation John must get absorbed in his protective stance, focused on not falling to the sharks. Through this intense activity, the voice of the speaker fades far into the distance. Mary can't be heard anymore.

What I told Mary:

1. Do your best not to threaten the end of a relationship in the heat of battle. Even if you're thinking, "I would be better off without you," as soon as you say that it raises the stakes and makes John unable to hear anything about the current issue.
2. Talk about behavior, no name-calling. Once you call John "useless" he can't hear you anymore. You could say, "You haven't picked up the kids from school or bought groceries in the past two weeks."

Solution

The emotional brain needs help staying out of the old groove. How can we help our lower brains out? We can become consciously aware of those old injuries by learning what childhood wounds trigger us to overreact. Next, we can feel tenseness in our bodies when the road threatens to pull us off course and actively intervene to stop our sled. You can stop the sled by breathing into the parts of your body where you're tensing up. This can help you avoid old unwanted patterns. As you become conscious in this way, you may be able to avoid even starting down the old path or at least shorten the ride by getting off the wrong path sooner.

Now let's return to our two examples:

<u>Mind/Body solutions for Anne who was criticized by her boss:</u>
Anne learned that even constructive criticism reminds her of being trapped as a child having to endure negative criticism from her parents. She realizes she may overreact even from milder constructive criticism. Next, she feels in her body the sled going down the old road. Then she breathes in her belly to lessen her anxiety. She reduces her anger by relaxing her jaw and moving it around. She sits up straight and pushes her feet into the ground to feel more settled.

<u>Mind/Body Solutions for John who was criticized by his wife:</u>
John learned that being called useless in the present reminds him of being called useless as a child and the name-calling triggered his fear of rejection. In his body, he puts his hand on his midsection and breathes into his diaphragm. (That's where he felt the "blow to his body.") He sits up straighter and presses his back against the chair to feel more present.

In the next chapter, I'll examine the body's role in listening and walk you through some exercises to help in any listening situation, by creating a new and more effective trail to sled down.

Take Aways:

1. For fast communication results, practice the 6 tools of active listening including this method for acknowledging what you hear: paraphrase, clarify and give feedback.

2. For the highest chance of success, review the 12 listening blocks before practicing the active listening method.

3. Whole brain listening means bringing together the UPPER (thinking) and LOWER (emotional) parts of the brain in service of best listening practices.

4. Under severe stress our LOWER brain focuses on survival and we can't think well which interferes with active listening.

5. Only in calming the LOWER brain can the UPPER brain regain power and help us listen. Practice the 6 tools for calming the emotional brain.

6. Past trauma can cause us to overreact. It creates pathways in the brain that put the LOWER brain in survival mode interfering with thinking. We must find safety and calm before new positive roads can be built.

7. Re-train your brain by using mind/body solutions to avoid going down old worrisome roads and find the calm road for good communication.

CHAPTER SIX

Gain Mastery at Listening to Difficult People

"I don't know why but I just can't stand him!"

You've probably heard or said something like this at one point. We all know what it's like to find yourself interacting with a person who irritates you or just plain rubs you the wrong way. It might be the way they sound or act, or truth be told, you may not even fully understand why you're experiencing such a negative reaction to this person. Nonetheless, when they speak, chances are the communication is not going to flow easily. You'll likely experience some sort of block, attempt to end the communication altogether or in the worst case find it escalating into a fight. But your communication with that person doesn't have to follow that pattern. With a bit of awareness and a simple technique you may find that a person who once distressed you no longer carries that power. In this chapter I'll have you look at:

- Why you may be having that specific response.
- How you can find a way to be less triggered.
- A body technique you can use to improve your listening to difficult people.

Tone Matters

There's an innate reason humans like pleasant sounding voices and recoil from harsh voices. We naturally move toward soothing, loving and happy tones of voice. We naturally move into a defensive space or feel unsafe when we hear angry, harsh or cold voices. Why? Historically this was a way for human beings to assess their safety. Tone of voice could illuminate if the person speaking was a predator or a friend. If the tone was dangerous it was time to fight or flee. If the voice was from a soothing caretaker it was time to bond for nurturing and sustenance. To help us, our ears are trained to pick up the nuance of safety or danger in vocal sounds. This is why we often turn away from voices that are harsh or otherwise unpleasant such as tones that are whiny, needy, grumpy, smothering, oppressive, creepy or cold and/or unfeeling. All this history is stored in our bodies. Practically, this means our bodies may need time to adapt and adjust after hearing an unpleasant tone of voice. Here's an example.

I'm writing this passage from the backyard of my room at a nature retreat center. I can hear birds chirping, bees buzzing, a hawk cawing in the distance and even some coyotes barking as a group. For a split second, as the coyotes' squeals get louder, I freeze. I find my thoughts running rapidly. *How close are they to me? Am I safe? Do I need to go back inside?* Before I move, I remind myself that this is a natural reaction from my body to become alert and quickly assess danger. As the sounds subside, I remember I'm used to hearing them daily and I relax again.

Negativity Bias

Negativity bias describes the phenomenon that unpleasant emotions, thoughts, events or social interactions have a bigger effect on our psychological state than do positive or even neutral emotions, thoughts or interactions. In plain language, we tend to focus more on negative thoughts and experiences over the positive much of the time. The biological reason for this is that negativity can signal danger and we need to stay alert to danger to stay alive.

If those coyote sounds had gotten closer, I would have needed to scamper inside quickly for safety. Rick Hanson in his book *Buddha's Brain* articulates how attention to the negative can color our ability to listen:

"Our brain colors experiences with a feeling tone: pleasant, unpleasant or neutral. We approach what is pleasant, avoid the unpleasant and move on from the neutral. We evolved to pay great attention to unpleasant experiences... However, this 'negativity bias' that primes you for avoidance overlooks good news, highlights bad news and can create anxiety and pessimism. When people spend too much time in anxiety, it is like they are always scanning for danger, which leaves little time to go inward for self-awareness and reflection. This negativity bias can highlight past failures, downplay present abilities and exaggerate future obstacles."

Resistance and Guilt

Understanding the natural pull toward protection from negativity can make us feel less guilty when we're not inclined to listen to others with kind thoughts. A history with someone who has been unpleasant can make us biased in a negative way, even when that person seems harmless today. This is an important concept because the more you become aware of your resistance, the more you can be in control of open hearted listening, even if you perceive a person to be negative or annoying.

Take this example where two people have different views of a person they both know. I find my mother-in-law very pleasant and loving. She calls me by a cute nickname and is always supportive and excited to be with me. She shares enthusiasm for many of the same activities I like, such as nature hikes, sculpting, painting, drawing, spontaneous swing dancing, spirituality and writing poetry. Every time I get off the phone with her, she ends the call telling me how blessed she is to have so much love and happiness in her life. No matter what I've been going through, after those calls I always experience a sense of peace, warmth and love wash over me, which makes me feel happy and grateful to have her in my life. Consequently, it's difficult for me to understand why someone wouldn't like her.

In stark contrast, one of her sons experiences her as anxious and smothering. This perception stems from relationship dynamics they had when he was a child. While growing up, he experienced his mother as smothering, which would often make him feel nervous and uncomfortable. Though many years have gone by and they no longer share that same dynamic, when she calls him up just hearing his mother's voice can make his shoulders hunch and his stomach tighten. Her voice may trigger him and unconsciously he's diving into a mini-movie in his head replaying their old interactions and how distressed it made him feel as a child. Consequently, he sometimes finds talking to her and being with her an unpleasant experience. He's experiencing negativity bias.

Body Technique for Listening to Difficult People

Let's say you have someone in your life who you find unpleasant or annoying and you'd like to be able to experience less annoyance. Or perhaps you'd like to avoid them but they happen to be a family member or co-worker so in some way or another, you have to learn to deal with them. The good news is that there are techniques to help you manage your reactions and at the risk of sounding too optimistic, you may even find a way to enjoy their company. Here are a few techniques that may help.

Release the Block: A Body Exercise
In the following exercise, you can locate and release a block to listening in your body.

1. Look at and place your hand on your belly. Next, breathe deeply in your belly by pushing your belly out when you inhale and relaxing your belly when you exhale.
2. Close your eyes and think of someone you don't like, respect or don't want to listen to. It's okay to acknowledge that you have trouble feeling empathy or compassion for this person.
3. Now imagine this person is talking to you and that it's your job to listen.
4. Take a moment to become aware of the emotions you're feeling. As you breathe, begin to notice any sensations you may feel in your body. Can you locate an area of tension (e.g. throat, jaw, fists, belly, shoulders)?
5. If practical, place your hand on that part of the body where you feel tense and press or massage the area. Now imagine the speaker once more.
6. Breathe into your tense body part as you press harder to help release some tension. Imagine your breath flowing to this tense area, relaxing the muscle.
7. RESULT: Tension is the body's way of holding back some emotional expression. Once you release the physical tension, the emotions will want to come out. The

emotions can be recognized and released if needed. Releasing feelings such as fear or hurt will help you feel better. Once you're aware of your emotions beneath the negativity, it can lead to more understanding, insight and relief.

A personal example: After designing this exercise I did it myself. Here's what I found. I thought of someone I have difficulty listening to. I imagined listening to her and noticed my eyes getting hard and my jaw tightening. I pressed my fingers on my jaw to release some of the tension. This made me cry a little. With the release of crying came the realization of how this person makes me feel as if I'm in the same position I was in as a child, when I sometimes felt pushed aside and dismissed as unimportant.

After doing this exercise I was better able to understand how this speaker "pushed my buttons." My ears were blocked to her because she provoked an old childhood wound. However, with awareness of how I felt provoked, it became easier to separate the speaker from my childhood experience. I was more able to clearly see that she's not the same person from my childhood and I'm no longer the helpless child victim I once was.

The Imaginary Scissors: A Mental Exercise
Who or what do they remind you of?

1. Take a moment to think of a person you find annoying or troublesome.
2. Close your eyes and take a deep breath.

3. Ask yourself: Who does this person remind me of? Travel through the various people in your lifetime of experiences searching for who may have caused you some similar distress as the current annoying person. Flip through the list (your mother, father, sister, brother, an old bully at school, an angry teacher, a mean-spirited cousin) until you find a match. There's no hurry; allow it to come to the surface when the time is right.

4. Take another deep breath. As you do so picture an imaginary pair of scissors cutting the tie between the current person in your life and the person he or she reminds you of. As you exhale let go of the connection between these two people. See them float further and further away from each other. You may want to do this several times.

5. See the current person in your life in a new light. Now that he or she has been separated from the memory, place a picture of the person in your mind's eye in a certain color you like such as a light blue, lavender, pink or soft green.

The Good News

With awareness you can gain understanding and therefore become more conscious of how and why this person "gets to you." With new tools in your arsenal you may notice you're more able to listen with greater openness. Once you do so, you may find the traits you previously found negative are not so provocative and in some happy cases you may even discover that being around the person doesn't bother you as much as it once did.

Take Aways:
1. A person's tone of voice can trigger an innate reaction. It may bring you either toward a place of safety or defense. If you're triggered and in a defensive place this can greatly interfere with active listening.
2. Appreciating our natural bent toward negativity (also known as negativity bias) can help reduce guilt when we struggle with listening openly to difficult people.
3. Practicing a body technique to release a block allows you to locate, breathe into and release body tension related to resistance in listening.
4. Practicing a mental imaging technique can assist you in your everyday life when you may need to listen to and work with difficult people.
5. Awareness from these two techniques gives you understanding of how the current "difficult" person triggers memories of a difficult person in your past.
6. Understanding past triggers can sometimes soften the negativity toward the current person, allowing you to listen with more openness in the present.

CHAPTER SEVEN

Become Understood by Expressing Your Feelings with New Clarity

We All Want to Be Heard

It's true. We all want to be seen and heard. Yet oftentimes, when we think we're expressing ourselves clearly, others just don't seem to get what we're trying to say. Have you ever seen that look on someone's face where you can tell they didn't understand you? We end up feeling like we didn't get what we wanted from expressing ourselves. This can lead to frustration and misunderstanding.

So what can be done?

In this chapter I'll share some solutions including the benefits of self-disclosure, making our emotions our allies and connecting emotional awareness to body sensations. Finally, techniques for both expressing and containing anger, sadness and fear will be provided.

Self-Disclosure

The first tool we'll look at is called self-disclosure. What is it? Simply put, it means you reveal a bit of your personal feelings or opinions to the listener by opening up and sharing some of what's going on with you. Though this may feel uncomfortable you'll find benefits that can vastly improve your life.

Four Benefits of Self-Disclosure

1. Self-disclosure encourages reciprocal communication. When we share something true about ourselves it invites those we're talking with to open up about themselves. Disclosure breeds disclosure. Communication then improves because more significant and personal topics are on the table. If I go deeper and say something personal about myself, others often will respond on a more personal level as well.

2. In close relationships, revealing information about yourself can lead to deepened intimacy. Sharing how you're feeling leads away from a shallow interaction and moves you toward a place where intimacy is

possible. You may find that your partner will more likely open up in response to your openness, which intensifies the closeness.

    a. Example from texting: "I'm bored and lonely here without you."

    b. Response from partner: "I miss you too."

3. Self-disclosure provides the benefit of increased energy. Holding onto a secret is stressful and can weigh you down energetically. When you reveal the secret you often feel a sense of relief, of lifting a burden.

4. Self-disclosure provides release from guilt and shame. Talking out loud can help you clarify how you feel, increasing self-understanding. Revealing something shameful may feel like a confession. You might have been carrying a load of guilt, shame and personal judgment. It's a great relief to find out that as you share others are often less judgmental than you may have expected. They may even be inclined to forgive you.

How to Know, Own and Express: Learn the Art of APE

APE stands for:

Awareness
Possession
Expression

In order to self-disclose clearly we first need to become aware of our feelings. One way to acknowledge our feelings is by recognizing where we feel them in our body. Knowing the feeling then leads to self-possession. To possess means to anchor the feeling, to own it and to have understanding and acceptance of our emotional state. Once we own it we can then decide how best to express our emotional state. Let's look at these three in detail. The first tells you ways to become aware of feelings.

AWARENESS of the Self

- Become aware of the primary (anger, sadness, fear, joy) feeling.
- Become aware of how strong the feeling is.
- Check for any possible secondary (guilt, shame, jealousy) feelings.
- Use your senses to tell you what your feeling is.

You know what? It may sound strange but emotions can be our friends. That's because in some way they reflect a true feeling from the depth of our being. If I feel hurt, even if I don't like that feeling and am more sensitive than I wish to be, then it's my job to at least notice that hurt feeling. This is true for all emotions, the major ones being sadness, anger, fear and joy. Most other feelings are close to one of those four.

Within those four main feelings you can go from a mild to a severe level. For example, have you noticed with anger you can be mildly annoyed or full of rage? With fear you can be slightly anxious or full-on terrified.

Here are some examples of possible feeling states on a continuum from low on the left to high on the right.

Anger continuum:
Mild irritation → annoyance → moderate anger → rage

Fear continuum:
Mild anxiety → worry → moderate fear → terror

Some feelings carry extra or secondary feelings such as guilt, shame or jealousy. The important thing is to become aware of what you're feeling and notice how mild or intense the feeling is. *How do I become aware of these various emotions?*

Neutral

Angry

Sad

Scared

Use Senses to Notice Emotions
People have different types of radar for knowing their emotions. Let's take awareness of anger, for example. Some of us

are **visual** so we may see an image of ourselves breaking something. That image may be the clue that alerts us to our anger. Are you more visual? I remember once when I was angry while doing the dishes, that I pictured smashing a cup on the floor. That image alerted me to my anger. Others of us may be more **kinesthetic** and notice in our bodies when we feel anger, perhaps by sensing that we're gritting our teeth, glaring with our eyes or noticing our fists balled up.

Which senses do you use?

Your senses are sight, hearing, touch, taste and smell. If you don't know which sense is more dominant for you, pay attention the next time you feel anger building. For example, do you visualize a reaction or hear yourself yelling? The good news is that the sooner you realize you're angry, the sooner you can choose how to act instead of the other way around, where the anger is in charge of your actions. This is true of the other emotions as well. The sooner I know I'm sad or scared, the sooner I can direct my reaction. Here's an example of a kinesthetic (touch) awareness of anger. Notice what happens when Rick becomes aware of his emotions.

Rick's Soccer Anger Story

Rick was playing a game of adult soccer when the same player fouled him for the third time in a half hour. He felt an impulse to go over to the offending player and push him to the ground or punch him. He could feel his hands balling up into a fist. He's an athlete and fairly aware of his bodily sensation so he recognized his anger rising. Because he was aware, he was able to immediately talk himself down instead of heading over to the player and punching him or throwing him down. Rick's awareness of his feelings helped him avoid a fight.

Sometimes we're not clear about our emotional state. We may be confused, lost in our head or somehow resistant to face our feelings. *Where might that resistance come from?* To get clues just think back to how your family handled emotions while you were growing up. For example, some feelings may have been more acceptable in your family than others. Bonny, a client of mine, found that she can cry easily but rarely expresses anger because in her family it was frowned upon. Another client, Kevin, on the other hand, found he had no trouble accepting his anger but found the vulnerability of sadness unacceptable. In his family, sadness was seen as weakness. Like Bonny and Kevin are you more comfortable with some feelings over others? Once we recognize which ones we're uncomfortable with we can move on to owning those feelings.

POSSESSION of the Self

Owning that *this feeling is truly mine* leads to self-possession. To possess a feeling is to have:

- An accepting point of view that your feeling has a right to exist.
- Some compassion about this emotion that's in you at this time.

For example, when Rick became aware of how angry he was getting he could have thought, "That guy is a jerk and no one gets to treat me that way."

Instead he thought, "That guy is a jerk, I'm mad and I have every right to be mad but I need to decide if I'm going to let that guy get the better of me."

Accepting the feeling inside can help you to tolerate the way it feels. For example, as you feel your anger you may notice and accept in your body the strength from your aggressive impulse to strike out.

Knowing, tolerating and possessing what you feel allows you to have some control over the next step: *How, if and when to express those feelings.*

EXPRESSION of the Self

Expression of feelings means moving the affect (or emotion) from the inside to the outside in an active way. In this section I'll define what anger, sadness and fear look like in the body and techniques for discharging (expressing) or containing those emotions.

Sometimes it's good to let the feelings flow outward

There are times when feelings need to be contained or soothed rather than discharged or expressed outwardly. We all know you can't yell back at a mean teacher or coach without getting in trouble. You might just have to endure their unkind words and not respond. However, there can be value in letting your feelings out at times. *So when is the right time?* One way to tell is if you're so unhappy that you feel your joy in life is diminished. Now with the teacher, you may not be able to yell back but later you might tell your parents how angry you felt. Your joy might return once you share your situation with them.

Here's an everyday story that reveals a missed opportunity to feel more joy.

Nadia's Late Arriving Sister Story

Nadia's sister Sharon was supposed to get to the pub early to save a table near the live band for their group on a crowded Saturday night. Sharon, however, arrived later than the rest of the group and the entire party had to wait over an hour for a table that was way in the back of the room. Nadia felt angry with her sister but didn't tell her. She found that the amount of fun she usually had with this sister was lessened because she didn't want to risk expressing her annoyance.

In the next section you'll learn practical ways to both express and contain anger, sadness and fear. First, let's discuss containment or why you might want to hold back from expressing your emotions. I mean if emotions contribute to our feeling of being alive and full of the joy of life, why hold back? The reason is that you may need to cool down from anger that's too hot, for fear of hurting someone or doing something destructive. Or you may need to hold back from expressing sadness if it's not the right time and/or place. For example, wailing uncontrollably during someone else's wedding vows because you're still hurting from your divorce might ruin the moment for the bride and groom. Or if you're hiking with a young child and you both see a scary snake in the path, you may have the urge to scream. Yet you may realize your scream would scare the child so you do your best to model courage. In that case, you might keep that scream inside while you scoop up the child and get out of the way. Having said all that, there are appropriate times and places to let your feelings out. Let's take a look at safe ways of getting our anger out and then ways of containing anger.

Looking at Anger in the Body

Imagine you're furious. Now imagine paying attention to the signals your body is sending you that tell you that you're angry. You might sense in your body when you feel your jaw getting tighter or your brow getting furrowed. You may also experience increasingly rapid breathing or gritted teeth. Whatever you notice, once you've decided to let it out, here are some effective and appropriate ways to do so.

Useful Tools for Letting Anger Out

Telling Someone

You can simply express that you feel angry by saying, "Hey, I'm mad at you." For example, Nadia, from the story above could have owned how she felt. She could have said, "I want to have fun with you tonight but I'm annoyed that you didn't get here early to get us a table like you promised." Her sister most likely would have apologized and Nadia would have forgiven her. The burden would then be gone and Nadia could have enjoyed her sister's company better.

Moving It Out of the Body

Children are naturally less able to contain their emotions than adults. It's normal for them to scream or throw a tantrum. While we may want to scream or throw a tantrum, these are less acceptable adult behaviors. Even though your body might feel relief from letting go of the pent-up anger by screaming and throwing a tantrum, you may escalate the situation in an unwanted way or create more chaos than you want. But that doesn't mean you can't get your feelings out of your body. In fact, any action that's safe for you and moves your body away from the scene of anger can help. If possible, find a way to go off alone (so you don't injure anyone or yourself) and do some form of vigorous exercise that you know you can do safely yet would push your body. For example, you might want to take a run or go to the gym. You could also scream in a (stopped) car or into a pillow. You know your body and its limitations. Think about what might be a powerful release that works for you. *The reward?* It feels good and you may experience immediate relief. You'll be getting rid of pent-up anger without hurting anyone or without making the situation worse. You may find that once you get it all out, you feel calmer or more neutral about the situation. Calming down from anger takes you back to the GREEN zone (see Chapter Four) where you can now communicate from a more thoughtful place.

The Supreme Importance of Containing Anger

The other option besides letting it out in a safe way is to allow the anger to cool down. When we feel we might be in danger of hurting someone our anger is too hot and we need to consider stepping away. Here's a useful way to contain anger even after you may have flared into expressing your anger.

The "Time-out" Technique

We all know about taking a "time-out" as usually it refers to a technique used with children. It allows kids to take a break and be separated from the family for an agreed upon time when they've misbehaved. But time-outs can be useful for all of us. All a time-out means is walking away from a heated moment when you know you'll most likely escalate the situation in the next few minutes. You may notice you're cussing, or getting louder, or throwing things or even pushing or hitting. This is a good moment for a time-out. (Ideally, it's better to take before any physical pushing or hitting). Merely tell your partner that you need a time-out. Use an agreed upon signal such as the "T" sign used in sports time-outs. (See the time-out sign with hands). This will tell your partner you're taking a break.

Choose an exact amount of time for the break (usually 20 minutes to an hour) and tell the person you're angry with that you'll return after that time to continue the discussion or to set a different time to talk. The other person MUST let you go and must agree not to follow you. This technique creates the time needed to cool down from dangerous levels of anger that could otherwise escalate quickly and create physical or emotional damage to people or property. As we know, the news is full of crimes by people hurting those they love while in fits of rage. This simple time-out technique could be one way to help save lives.

When Anger is a Secondary Emotion

Sometimes anger is the emotion we notice because it's right on the surface, yet truth be told, there may be something else going on with us. There are times when anger, as red and loud as it can be, is covering up an entirely different emotion such as fear, sadness, hurt, shame, guilt or embarrassment.

Why is it important to know what's beneath the anger?

Let's say you feel the anger and you express the anger. But if sadness is what's really going on then you may not feel better even after getting the anger out. The sadness would still be sitting there waiting to be recognized.

You may feel more in control expressing your anger but you won't feel satisfied until you become aware of and cope with the primary emotion behind your anger. The next story illustrates the futility of rage when anger is hiding another feeling.

<u>Hailey's Nasty Divorce Court Battle</u>

Hailey was fueled by vengeance. Her husband Tom, it turns out, had been having an affair and the two were having it out in divorce court. Hailey spent most of her days finding ways to discredit and disparage Tom to the judge, to their grown children and to their mutual friends. One day Hailey sunk down in her chair and revealed to her friend, "Under all of this rage, I'm just really heartbroken."

And there it was. All the anger that fueled the vicious fighting in divorce court was a secondary emotion to the sad heartbreak she felt at the breakup of her marriage.

Best Ways for Managing Hurt and Sadness

You may recognize hurt and/or sadness when you notice that your heart or an area in your chest feels heavy or weighed down. Here's how I think about it. When we have unexpressed sadness, our lungs are like buckets getting heavier as they fill with the weight of more and more water. I think that's because we feel dragged down by the weight of unshed tears.

<u>Letting Sadness Out to Feel Better</u>

Have you ever noticed your eyes stinging, your jaw quivering or a lump in your throat forming as you fight your body's impulse to cry? The tears want to flow but you've decided to hold them back. Maybe you don't want to cry in front of co-workers or family. And in some cases that might be the best option.

On the other hand, crying can often be the cure for unexpressed sadness. When we hold back tears, we may remain tense. Some people fear crying, avoiding it in any way they can. However, holding it in may result in a longer-term issue like anxiety or depression. So crying (at the right place and right time) might be the best option for expressing sadness, grief or hurt.

What if crying scares you? What if you think you might lose control if you start crying? What if you fear you may never stop? You might need someone to support and reassure you as was the case with Maria, a client dealing with the death of her baby. She told me that if she cried she feared she would go crazy. So she avoided crying at all costs. We talked it over and discussed the possibility that she may not go crazy when she cries, that maybe that thought was mistaken or distorted. She let what I said sink in. Then she took a risk and began to cry. I was there to support her. Not long after that cry, her fear flowed away down the river with her warm tears and she felt much better.

Released tears contain stress hormones so even the body wants you to release them! That's why people usually feel better "after a good cry."

Learn When It's Best to Contain Sadness

I believe in emptying the bucket of tears when it fills up. However, as we discussed about anger, some situations may call for restraint. The only value in containing your expression of sadness is if the time or setting is inappropriate or you need to care for yourself or others. When you're able to find a time or place to allow your sadness to emerge, let it flow out of you. You can nurture yourself at that point - maybe by taking a long, slow walk in nature or walking with bare feet in grass or on a sandy beach. Being surrounded by nature sometimes offers solace when you need to let the sadness be felt.

Finding Fear in the Body

Fear varies in degrees from a quick mild scare (like that sudden loud popping sound you quickly realize is just a car backfiring) to full blown terror (a life-threatening attack on your body). Fear is a natural response to feeling you're in danger either physically or emotionally. The body reacts by automatically pulling away or withdrawing as a protective measure from the real or perceived danger.

A quick exercise: Take a moment to imagine that someone just yelled and it startled and scared you. Imitate an expression of fear and hold it in your body. Now freeze and hold your pose a few seconds. *What do you notice going on in your body?*

You may have noticed one or all of these responses:

- You took a quick in-breath in your chest and felt a sense of freezing up and tightness in your chest.
- You became still and watchful with open, alert eyes.
- You tightened your neck and pulled your upper body away in an attempt to withdraw.

These are some of the body's automatic responses to fear.

Effective Tools for Discharging Fear

Natural reactions to fear may be screaming, cowering, ducking or getting away by any means. But we can't always get away, even when the body has the impulse to do so. As a result, when the actual or perceived danger is over we're sometimes still holding onto that pent-up fear in our body. We may feel relieved that the danger has passed, yet our nervous system may still be in distress because we couldn't actually get away during the fearful event. Here's an example.

Brian's Story:

Brian was in English class when the usually mild-mannered teacher, Mr. Norman, threw down some papers and yelled at the class for doing so poorly on the most recent test. When Mr. Norman lost control like that, the students were taken aback and froze in their chairs.

Brian was relieved when Mr. Norman began to compose himself and pick up the papers he had thrown on the floor. But Brian's body was still on alert and he had trouble returning to a calmer state for the rest of the day.

When he got home, Brian noticed he was agitated and anxious.

He put on his running shoes and went for a long run in a nearby park. After a while he could feel the stress drain from his body.

BONUS NOTE: If you're anxious or stressed and don't know why, go back through your day and see if you can find anything that might have provoked your mood. *Did you have to contain an impulse to get away or escape?*

Good Ways to Move Fear Out
Here are some ways to move your body and let the fear out:
- Scream into a pillow with a high-pitched voice
- Shake your whole body like a ragdoll quickly so as to loosen it up

Note: Once the fear is discharged it may lead to anger which may also need to be expressed. This is because when we feel threatened, our brain sends signals to the body to activate flight (get away) or fight (take action to defend ourselves). So if the expression of fear leads to anger, then you can then decide how you want to manage the anger.

The Crucial Importance of Containing Fear
Calling attention to your fear may not be effective in some situations. In fact, it might activate a sadistic response from the person attacking you. As in the animal kingdom, appearing weak may motivate a predator to pursue his prey even more. To contain (hold back) the appearance of fear or to calm fear involves similar techniques.

Effective Ways to Contain Fear:

1. **Safety meditation**
   Place your hand on your belly, lean against the support of a chair or couch or lie down. Slowly breathe in and out until you calm down. Think of a place where you

feel safe and cozy (like a cushioned chair or your bed) while breathing slowly. You may want to squeeze and let go of a soft blanket (or a corner of your sweater) in rhythm with your breath to manage your fear until you feel more contained or calm.

2. Wall-sitting technique

Lean your back flat against a wall while standing. Bend your knees with your feet 12 inches in front of you. Imagine a safe and comfortable place where you feel relaxed. Breathe slowly into your lower body by pushing out your belly while you inhale and relaxing on the exhale.

Here's what happened one time when I used this tool:

Some years ago, I had to give my first all-day seminar on a new topic to an international audience. As I walked to the venue early in the morning, I found that I felt anxious and sick to my stomach. I slipped into the restroom before my presentation and did the following exercise. In the stall I leaned my back against the wall with my knees bent and feet one foot in front of me. I told myself I would either throw up or not and to accept what my body needed to do. I imagined being in my warm bed and did some slow abdominal and diaphragmatic breaths (see Chapter Two). Soon my nausea went away, I felt less fearful, and I went in and gave my seminar with no residual problems.

Summary: Self-disclosure reveals who we are at a level of depth that increases intimacy with others. Using APE, we can notice, possess and express or contain our feelings in productive ways.

Take Aways:
1. "Self-disclosure" reveals information about the self. It encourages others to open up, can increase self-knowledge, deepens intimacy, increases energy and relieves you of guilt and shame.
2. With awareness, possession and expression (APE), emotions become your allies in life.
3. Emotions manifest in body sensations. It's important to pay attention to these body clues.
4. You can use your senses to zoom in and learn about your emotional state.
5. Knowing, having acceptance of and compassion for feelings in the moment lead to self-possession. Self-possession gives you the power to control how you express your feelings.

6. Expressive exercises release pent-up emotions and free up your energy for happiness. Containing exercises help calm and center your body so you can decide how to best respond to emotional stimulation. Learn body tools for both expressing and containing each of these feelings: anger, sadness and fear.

CHAPTER EIGHT

Your Voice and a Pillow: The Cure for Stuffing Your Emotions

Connecting to your emotions can be powerful. It can also be difficult. In our everyday world, we often receive the message to contain or hide our emotions. We get insulted at work and we stuff it down. We get cut off in traffic and we stuff it down. Our partner makes a less than caring comment when we get home a little late and we stuff it down. What this constant "stuffing down" routine results in is a lot of repressed feelings. When we repress our feelings day after day, we don't even realize it but after a while we've trained ourselves to ignore our feelings altogether. The issue here is that our feelings don't just stay stuffed down and out of sight. Unexpressed emotions can cause all kinds of havoc like not sleeping, overeating, lack of interest in work or home life, illness, passive aggressive outbursts or straight up anger that erupts seemingly without our permission.

The key is to find safe and healthy ways to connect and release those emotions.

You may be surprised that the key to getting out those emotions is right in your bedroom. All you need is a willingness to use your voice and a pillow. Let me walk you through it.

Learn the Connection of Linking Sound with ALL the Emotions

Using your voice to express emotions can feel empowering. I've heard people exclaim after a strong vocal expression, "I feel more like myself now."

So, why is that? The word "person" comes from "per sona" meaning per sound or by the sound. By the sound, you know the person! By our sounds, we make ourselves heard. By the sound of our true emotions, we express the depth and heart of our true selves. Have you ever been on the phone and thought, "This person sounds happy (or sad or mad)" even if their words are not matching those emotions? When our voice and affect match we send a stronger more understandable message to others. In the following technique, we'll link emotion and sound to match the mad, sad, bad and glad emotions.

What's the benefit of expending energy to express emotions in this strong way? The unexpressed or blocked emotions you carry in your body and psyche weigh you down. Expression of affect reduces the burden, frees up your energy and allows you to feel lighter and happier. Even if you currently don't feel these emotions, this exercise can loosen the muscles related to freer expression. Even if it feels like acting, do it anyway. So, when you do feel these emotions, your body may remember how it felt and you might find it easier to express your feelings.

Sound Pillow Techniques to Loosen the Expressive Voice

All you need for this series of exercises is a pillow and some willingness to sound a little funny. We may feel somewhat silly at first because as adults we're not as expressive as when we were kids, so we're out of practice. When I use these techniques with clients, even though they're often hesitant, once they get started they get into it and find so much relief of tension as a result. I recommend you give these tools a go.

Mad Pillow Talk

This can feel a little weird at first but keep going as this technique can be quite effective. You were really good at this at age two. Your body just needs to remember!

- Think of something that annoys you about someone in your life right now. For example, it could be a driver who recently cut you off on the road.
- Notice and exaggerate any bodily expression by tightening your fists, baring your teeth, bringing your lower jaw forward or letting anger out through your eyes, staring in a threatening way at your object of anger.
- Next, grab a pillow and growl loudly into the pillow. Growl as loud and as long as you can. If you feel a strain in your throat, back off and don't growl as hard. Then do it again.
- You could also yell, "No" loud and long into the pillow. Afterward, see how you feel. If anger is easy for you, you may have found that you enjoyed this technique. If anger is hard for you, congratulations; you may have loosened some muscles and begun opening up your voice. This can make expressing your anger easier when you need it.

Sad Pillow Talk

- Take a pillow and press it into your chest while curling your sitting body over the pillow. Collapse your chest and drop your head.

- Next, imagine something that makes you sad, anything from a minor hurt to a major grief.
- Take a long slow breath and on the exhale moan into the pillow by saying, "Ohhhh" long and loud.
- After the next inhale, say "Oh, oh, oh."
- These sounds can open up the voice and loosen the diaphragm, which helps release sadness and perhaps tears. If your tears are activated, let yourself cry with sound.
- Experiment and stay with the sounds that most release sadness. If crying is tough for you, you might feel stuck. If so, just breathe. Take a break and do it again. The good news is that the more you do it, the easier it gets.

Fear Pillow Talk

- Recall a recent time when you were frightened.
- Bury your scared face deeply into the pillow and scream in a high voice all the way to the end of the out breath.
- Do this a few times until you can sustain the sound longer. Remind yourself that getting the scream through the voice is only to release the energy held by fear in the body. Doing it as completely as possible discharges the affect. If expressing fear reactivates a trauma or scary event and you feel stuck, it usually means the affect is not completely released. Continue breathing and trust that your body wants you to heal from the trauma.

NOTE of caution: If you start to feel too anxious as you do this exercise, it may indicate that you're feeling unsafe. Sometimes that means outside help to deal with your fears would work better. I strongly recommend therapy as a support to work with trauma or with moving out your fear or other emotions.

Happy Pillow Talk (Tossing the Happiness Pillow)

You can do this next exercise standing, sitting or lying down.

- Think of someone or something that makes you happy.
- Hold the pillow above your head with both arms. Look up and smile at the pillow as you recall that happy joyful time.
- Bring the pillow back close to your face. Slowly push the pillow up and then toss it in the air above your head as you smile and say, "ha-ha-ha-ha-ha-ha-ha (until the end of your exhale).
- Catch the pillow and do this over and over until perhaps some spontaneous laughter occurs. The key to laughing is loosening the diaphragm. If you're having a hard time, contract the diaphragm more when you make the "ha-ha-ha" sounds. Do the best you can to be in the moment and enjoy tossing your happiness pillow.

BONUS NOTE: It's difficult to fully enjoy happiness if we're carrying blocked sadness, fear or anger. So if joy isn't coming to you in the happiness pillow toss, I recommend you go back and do the mad, sad, bad pillow tools first. You'll be pleased to find that once those tougher emotions are released you'll have so much more room for joy!

Take Aways:

1. Using your voice to clearly express your repressed emotions can be healthy and empowering.
2. Sound pillow exercises can loosen the expressive voice, which releases throat tension and restores a balanced feeling in the body and psyche.
3. Growling or yelling, "No" into a pillow can move out blocked anger so you don't have to carry it around.
4. Pressing a pillow over your chest and making long moaning "Oh" sounds can open up a blocked expression of sadness.
5. Opening your eyes and screaming in a high voice into a pillow can release blocked fear.
6. Smiling and using laughing sounds while tossing a pillow can make you feel happy, especially if you've previously released stuck fear, anger or sadness.

CHAPTER NINE

The Magic Power of Whole Messages

If you were forced to choose only one tool from this book, I promise you that whole messages would be your best choice. *Why?* Because in the world of expressing yourself, when you use a whole message you're being so thorough that it's nearly impossible not to be understood. If you are misunderstood, it will be the fault of the listener due to some listening block. We can't control others but we can use our best tools and this is the finest jewel in the expression box. So come learn the magic power of whole messages. Some of the history of the concept can be found in the reference section at the end of the book.

<u>What's the big deal?</u>

Whole messages connect the body, the emotions and the thinking brain to assist the speaker in creating the best request or response when strong communication is needed. Here's an illustration.

Imagine you're taking a timed test in school. This test determines whether you'll qualify to become licensed in your chosen field. The teacher walks through the classroom and pauses to look over your shoulder. She hovers there. You want to hide or say something but somehow you feel like you can't. Your focus is on her. You may feel annoyed. You may find it becomes hard to concentrate or think clearly. You may find all you can think of is your desire for her to leave now! Once she does, you sigh and find you can concentrate once more.

Wouldn't it be nice to have a technique to communicate your emotions and get the thinking brain back online sooner, especially as in this story if the test is timed? This is where the great technique of whole messages can come to your rescue. We'll return to this example at the end of this section to see how to address the test-hovering-teacher anxiety by using our newly honed whole messages response.

<u>Diving into Whole Messages</u>

Whole messages refer to expressing yourself in a complete way leaving nothing out. *How does it work?* Ideally, before an important communication you write out the four parts of the whole message and fill in the details. You can have your notes with you to help, whether the talk is on the phone or in person. If it seems strange to have notes for a live discussion, see if you can memorize your points. However, memorizing can put extra stress on the thinking brain, which may not be very strong in times of emotional arousal. The written notes help contain your emotions and return you to your best thinking. This is especially important in high stakes communication where being heard correctly may be crucial to your success. *What are the four aspects that complete a whole message?*

THE FOUR PARTS OF A WHOLE MESSAGE:

1. Observations or facts (actual behaviors you notice)
2. Thoughts or beliefs (may involve your philosophy or value system)
3. Feelings/Emotions (I feel...must be followed by YOUR emotion: disclose your anger, hurt, fear or other emotion)
4. Wants or needs (may refer to action by you or action of the listener)

You may find it easiest to have each of the four parts begin with the word "I." For example, "I see; I think; I feel; I need." This helps you own your view. Do your best not to start with the word "You..." as it moves the conversation toward blaming the other, which may turn him or her off to listening.

What might this look like? We'll start with an example that has low stakes like wanting cookies someone brought to the office.

Example: Correct
1. I see you brought a box of cookies to the office.
2. I think sharing is a nice thing to do.
3. I feel a craving for the chocolate chip cookies I see there.
4. I would like a cookie. Can I have one?

This is a simple non-conflictual example to show the use of starting with "I" statements. You could just as easily have asked, "Can I have a cookie?"

But even in these simple moments of communication we can be ineffective and misunderstood.

Example: Incorrect
1. Oh, cookies! Where did you come from?
2. You don't need those.
3. You aren't going to eat all those yourself, are you?

These are "you" statements. The listener doesn't know if you want a cookie or not. And missing is the fourth part: stating your want.

The listener could ignore the speaker if they wished because no request was made. In fact, when one part (of the necessary four parts) is left out it's called a "partial message."

The Danger of the Partial Message

Partial messages leave out one or more parts of the **whole** message, opening the door to misinterpretation by the person listening to the message. In the following scenario the listener doesn't know what the speaker wants so the listener may be left unclear.

In this scenario the speaker will share:

1. Their observations,
2. Thoughts and
3. Feelings **but leave out the**
4. **Fourth part of a whole message: their wants or needs.**

Imagine the speaker is talking to you. Here's what can happen:

Scenario: Your partner enters the bedroom in the dark while you're in bed. What they really want is for you to turn on the light but this is what they say to you.

1. "I notice it's dark in here." (**fact**)
2. "I could bump into things in the dark." (**thought**)
3. "I'm scared I might bump into something." (**feeling**)

As the listener you don't know if the speaker plans to do anything or wants you to do something for them. If the speaker includes the fourth part of a whole message and ends with, "Please switch on the light" (**need**), then you'll know what they want you to do. An action they want has been clearly communicated. You have the option to comply or not but the communication is complete and you have no doubt about their intentions. At least you know what they want. The fourth part could also be, "I'll turn the flashlight on my cell phone to see better."

This tells you that your partner will take action and you don't need to do anything. Including that fourth part of either a request for your action or communicating his or her action completes the entire communication. This is an example of how a whole message can be clear and feel complete to the listener.

You might be thinking that stating your needs in this fashion might be too obvious. I've noticed in therapeutic situations that partners often wish their spouse knew what they wanted or offered to give them what they needed, without having to "spell it out." But, alas, others (even those who care for us deeply) are not mind readers! So be sure to include part 4: your needs and wants.

ALERT: The whole message technique can seem deceptively simple. The truth is it does take practice to master, so I invite you to spend some time practicing. Test it out at least three times in the next few weeks and see how it goes.

A Cautionary Tale:

I taught this technique to a client who was in conflict with her husband.

For 1) Facts/Observations: the client came up with, "We don't have a real marriage."

Is that a fact? The client thought it could be a fact. But this wasn't correct as the statement was an opinion and not a fact. It's further a generalized indictment that could set up a defensive response in the husband and crush the communication immediately. In this case a stronger fact/observation comment might include some of the **specific missing behaviors** which could be addressed. Here's a clearer example along with possible other parts of the whole message this client could have used:

1. We haven't been on a date in a year; we're not sleeping in the same bed; I notice you walk away when I want to talk about our issues.
2. I value having a strong marriage.
3. I feel hurt, lonely and frustrated.
4. I want to discuss going into marital counseling with you.

PRACTICE EXERCISE:

Take a moment to:

Think of someone you want to communicate with or are in a conflict with currently. Fill in the blanks using the whole message approach.

1) FACTS/OBSERVATIONS: "I notice that" (list your or their behavior)_____
2) **MY** THOUGHTS/BELIEF: "I believe that" (state your values or philosophy)_____
3) **MY** FEELINGS: "I feel" (write some EMOTION: any variation of sad, mad, glad or bad)_____
4) **MY** NEEDS/WANTS: "I need (or want)"... (for you, us or me to...state some action)_____

How did you do? Look back at the EXACT definitions of each part to improve. Practice by filling in blank spaces with another topic you would like to address in your relationships.

Short and Sweet 3-Part Communication

There's even a shorter version of the four-part whole message which only involves three parts. Granted, it leaves out the second step of sharing your viewpoint or opinion. The 3-part version is easier to use in simpler (where a whole message isn't needed) situations.

The 3-part message works best:

- When your opinion or values are not an important part of the discussion.
- In situations where it may not be appropriate to share your values or beliefs.
- If you feel stressed, your brain isn't clear and you must speak up soon.

The 3-part message looks like this:

FILL IN: (you're the speaker)

When you_____(state the listener's behavior).

*I feel_____(fill in the speaker's emotion- sad, mad, glad, scared).

And I want (to/you to)_____(fill in proposed speaker's action or listener's action).

*CAUTION: AGAIN, WATCH FOR THIS COMMON MISTAKE – DO NOT SAY, "I FEEL THAT YOU..." AS THIS IS USUALLY FOLLOWED BY YOUR OPINION JUDGING THE OTHER OR SOME FORM OF CRITICISM. THIS IS A TURN-OFF AND INVITES DEFENSIVENESS.

Here are three examples of the ineffective, "I feel that you…" and stronger versions using the short and sweet 3-part communication:

Example #1: When you want a depressed family member to get help.

Ineffective:
I feel that you're depressed and should go into therapy.

More effective 3-part communication:
1. When you stay in bed for three days
2. I worry about you
3. and I want you to consider getting outside help.

Example #2: When a roommate isn't pulling his or her weight and you want him or her to take action.

Ineffective:
I feel that you're lazy, stupid and disgusting.
(Name-calling makes others defensive)
Effective 3-part communication:
1. When you haven't kept your promises to help with chores
2. I feel bothered by that and
3. I need you to do the dishes before you go to bed tonight.

Example #3: When someone is late repaying a loan and you want him or her to pay you back.

Ineffective:
I feel that you need to pay me back.

Effective 3 Part Communication:
1. When you failed to pay me back the $100 loan you said you would pay back last month
2. I felt angry that you had not paid me nor said anything about it and
3. I want you to please give me the money you owe or talk to me about a payment plan today.

Story: Hovering Over Test Taker

We'll now return to the story of your brain going off-line under the pressure of being watched by your teacher while you take a crucial written test. Either one of these messages might solve the problem. You could use either the short 3-part version or the whole message to get through to this hovering teacher.

EFFECTIVE Short and Sweet 3-Part Version (leaving out your opinion):

1. When you watch me take this timed test,
2. I feel anxious and that interferes with my brain concentration, slowing my time.
3. I want you to please stop looking over my shoulder.

OR you can use a 4-part message to address this same issue like this:

4-Part Whole Message (always use this method for important conflictual situations):

1. You look over my shoulder during timed tests.
2. I think that interferes with my concentration, slowing down my time.
3. I feel self-conscious, then anxious and nervous and can't keep my mind on the test.
4. I would like to respectfully request that you not look over my shoulder during tests.

Expressing Your Feelings is BRAVE

I want to acknowledge that it's sometimes difficult to disclose emotions even though that may be the only way to reveal your true self to another and get the longed-for result of being understood. Yes, taking that step to disclose your feelings can be scary. Would you talk to a teacher about your feelings, as in the previous example? You may feel it's too risky. What if it backfires? What about revealing information about yourself to someone you care about? What if they shame or reject you?

It is a risk to disclose feelings when we feel vulnerable, don't feel safe or fear it might make things worse. We all have ways of talking that involve staying away from painful feelings. This is understandable. These defenses protect us from emotional pain and are part of our communication style, sometimes unconsciously. But staying quiet can backfire. You can hide but then you may end up feeling unheard, disconnected and lonely. Sometimes we may not even know we're hiding our feelings and are surprised when others are confused or hurt by our way of talking.

So it's important to face that you're very brave when you take the time to understand how you feel and even braver when you share those feelings. Note that using whole messages or the simpler 3-part message BOTH CONTAIN DISCLOSING **YOUR EMOTIONAL STATE** WITH THE LISTENER. Without that you won't be understood in conversations that involve your feelings. If you want to be understood, then you have to peel back your mask and let others see you. You can do it! Once you take the risk and it pays off you'll notice that it feels wonderful. It feels as if you've truly taken care of yourself.

This chapter has covered the crucial tool of using complete messages, a powerful technique that can help get your meaning across in a clear, concise and successful manner. Practicing 4-part or 3-part messages will increase your effectiveness at being heard.

Take Aways:

1. Speaking by using a "whole message" tool is optimal for complete verbal communication. Only a complete verbal message can guarantee the highest possibility of your being both heard and understood.

2. Whole messages include four parts: sharing your observations, thoughts, feelings and needs.

3. Partial messages leave out one part and are incomplete. This can make your meaning less clear.

4. A 3-part message leaves out your thoughts/opinions (which aren't always appropriate) but does include your observations, feelings and requests.

5. For important conversations and especially ones with conflict, write down the four parts of your message to insure covering all your points.
6. Practicing 3-part or 4-part messages will increase your skills with this crucial tool.

CHAPTER TEN

Ways to Stay Open in Order to Get Through Conflict

During a conflict, communication can be difficult because our impulse may be to pull in or push others away, especially in anger. In other words, when situations get heated we usually don't like to stay around so we look for a quick way out, either emotionally or physically. This usually involves fleeing or fighting. However, there's another approach that allows for more options, keeps us engaged and includes the possibility of a positive resolution. How can we

149

keep communication lines open when we're so angry that we don't want to stay in the arena? Learning about cold anger can lead to a solution. When you get so angry that you feel coldness then two-way communication has little hope for success. This chapter covers the concepts of cold and warm anger as well as how to use love as a resource, especially when listening to people who are in pain. Seven common mistakes for dealing with people in pain are followed by a compassionate listening recipe. I'll end with covering techniques for responding to criticism.

Cold and Warm Anger Zones

Has this happened to you? Someone's behavior angers you to the point that you feel you don't like them, don't want to engage with them, don't care about them and aren't interested in restoring any goodwill. What has happened is that your heart is (more or less) closed to them. It's common to have at least one family member, schoolmate or co-worker you feel this way about. When your heart is closed to restoring goodwill, you're carrying cold anger. You may not mind keeping some people out of your heart but what if you need to communicate with someone you feel cold toward? Then you have this problem: **Cold Anger Makes Communication Very Difficult or Nearly Impossible!**

But then let's say this person you need to talk to says something that warms your heart just a bit. Maybe her or she apologizes or self-discloses something that helps you understand the behavior that bothered you. Now you find yourself a little less angry. You feel softer and more open. Your ice-cold attitude begins to thaw as warmth fills your heart. Next, you feel an energetic shift where you have some interest in restoring good-will. This is the zone of warm anger which gives you this so-lution:

Warm Anger Makes Communication Easier and More Possible!

Put another way, cold anger doesn't seek to reach out toward the other person while warm anger does seek to connect in some way with the other person.

This chapter will help you identify when you're experiencing cold or warm anger. It will also teach you how to move yourself gently from cold to warm anger. Only when anger is warm can you reach out successfully.

First, let's learn a bit more about the types of anger we experience.

When is it Cold or Warm?

Anger is cold → when we feel we have no hope of being seen or heard by someone.

Anger is warm → when we seek to restore a good feeling in a relationship.

What happens to cold anger if we leave it unattended? It can turn to rage as we get bitter and (though we may deny it) seek revenge or power over the person who has offended us. Is there anyone in your life who brings up feelings of deep bitterness or rage? Chances are you'll be in a state of cold anger when and if you need to communicate with this person.

Have you ever given up on someone and settled into a place of staying superficial or being distant? You may be fine with that decision and feel that limiting contact allows you to have the healthy boundaries you need. If this person isn't an active part of your life it may not be a problem. But if the person is in your life actively, for example, your ex-spouse or a hard-to-deal-with co-worker, then you may need some tools to keep communication open.

What happens to warm anger? It rests in a place of possibility because even though you feel mad, some part of you really wants to connect and communicate. Since you still hope to be seen and heard, there's hope to break through and decrease the emotional distance.

Is there anyone in your life who you're angry at yet some part of you wants to rekindle your closeness? You may be wondering how you can reach out to him or her when much of you is feeling you want to pull away. The first step is to find out what your body does when you pull your heart in. But heed this warning first.

Warning:

Is there ever a time not to reach out? Yes, when you're in an *unhealthy* relationship such as when you're the victim of physical abuse, emotional abuse or neglect. In these cases, reaching out may endanger you or others. Self-disclosing your true feelings to someone you know to be untrustworthy or volatile may not be safe. Sharing your vulnerability needs an environment of safety. In these cases, you may end up feeling like you're taking better care of yourself not to reach out. Your safety should always be considered and for self-protection you should gauge your level of danger.

However, a third party such as a therapist may be helpful to mediate in a conflictual relationship where trust and safety are issues, especially with couples. Another time not to reach out is when the anger dissipates by itself and you no longer feel annoyed. The clue to knowing whether or not you need to deal with an issue is to check in and see if you're still bothered (angry) and if there's potential (a healthy relationship) for healing the rift.

Revenge is often a natural inkling when we're angry or feel betrayed. It's motivated by an urge to hurt the other person but it's not a good incentive for reaching out and will not restore peace. So, proceed ONLY IF you feel safe and wish to restore a good relationship with a person who has the potential to hear your messages.

The Reaching Technique: Love as a Resource
The following exercise shows you how a cold or warm heart affects the body in highly different ways. Let's start by locating these noticeable physical changes in your body.

<u>Discover How Reaching Feels in the Body</u>
1. Think of someone who has recently (or in the past) rejected or hurt you. Now reach with your arms as if reaching toward that rejecting/hurtful person. Notice where you feel restrictions or a reluctance in your body.

    List those bodily restrictions:_____
    _____

    Example: When I reach toward_____ (someone you don't like) I feel "my chest tighten, arms stiffen, eyes deaden/or look suspicious, my mouth form into a tense smile and I lean away slightly with my shoulders and back." (Note any body reactions. There may be many or just one.) Next, close your eyes, drop your arms and breathe.

2. Now, picture someone in your current world who loves you. It can be a person or a beloved pet. Reach with your arms toward this loving being. Notice your body reactions.

   List your bodily response:_____

   Example: When I reach toward_____(someone who loves you) I feel "my jaw loosen, smile broaden, eyes brighten, arms get warm and my chest takes deep, slow breaths that seem to fill me with joy." Take notice of how good you feel in your body reaching toward love when you're confident the other person will respond warmly.

   Keep these positive feelings as a resource to use when you're dealing with people in pain (or people who are a pain). It's like the love you feel fills up your body to make you feel more solid. Coming from a place of love, you're standing on a more stable base which counteracts the negative feelings. Being able to access these positive feelings will help you to feel less reactive or defensive and more open and tender hearted. As a result, you're more likely to feel like your heart is open and present.

Practice Using Love As A Resource

Being able to access a present heart takes practice. Anytime you're feeling cold-hearted you can use the exercise of reaching toward a beloved person to help transform the way you feel and react.

The next time you're faced with someone who's a pain to you or is in pain (or both), close your eyes and imagine reaching toward and being warmly received by someone who loves you (as in the previous exercise). It could be the memory of your child or grandchild running into your arms, your spouse giving you a big hug or your puppy wagging his tail excitedly. Choose the memory that brings you the biggest smile. Reliving this memory, even briefly, can make you feel better able to hang in there during a painful interaction.

Compassion as a Way of Being: Learning from Nurses

In a psychiatric hospital I watched an angry scared patient with dementia be bossy and mean to two different nurses. I looked at the nurses' faces and was amazed how they "took it in stride." They just smiled and kept working. I imagine they were used to that kind of treatment and had learned to tolerate it. However, understanding and compassion may also help to keep their hearts open and not react in a negative way. As I watched them work, I thought about the "love as a resource" exercise. I felt that in some way, consciously or unconsciously, these amazing nurses were coming from a place of love to help them get through this difficult work shift.

Compassionate Listening: When the Speaker is in Pain

The first step of a compassionate response is to listen to the other person and let him or her know you're listening, especially to his or her feelings. However, the truth is that we all (from time to time) make some of the following seven common mistakes when we're responding to people in pain. Notice the unintended results that may happen because of the mismanaged communication. *Which have you used?*

7 Common Communication Mistakes While Listening to People in Pain:

1. **Minimizing or Discounting Feelings.** The doctor says, "Oh, there are patients here with worse conditions than yours." This may be an attempt at offering, "You'll survive this" but this approach can make the patient feel more terrified as well as discounted. "Don't worry," "Calm down," "You're overreacting," and "There's nothing to be afraid of," are attempts at reassurance that minimize or discount the speaker's feelings. This doesn't work because *talking people out of their feelings only increases their sense of isolation and pain.*

2. **Giving Advice.** Offering helpful (and unsolicited) advice and suggestions both cuts off the feelings and indicates that you don't believe the speaker can solve their own problems. *Consider advising only when the speaker asks for advice.*

3. **Interrogating.** This happens when we ask too many questions when gathering information for problem solving. By asking so many questions, you may appear uninterested in the speaker's pain. You may be in a role where you need to ask questions to gather information but shouldn't do so with a *tone of disinterest when it comes to the speaker's pain.*

4. **Blaming.** This is what people do when they blame the speaker who may be a victim. For example, Karen told Janice she thought that Janice's pregnancy losses were Janice's fault because she smoked. *Blaming the victim tells them they deserve their pain.*

5. **Deflecting.** As a person begins to express pain, deflecting happens when you make a joke or change the subject to something less painful. Though there may be some giggling which can sometimes be a welcome relief, *deflecting gives the speaker the message that you can't or don't want to cope with their pain.*

6. **Justifying or Explaining.** In this defense, because you're unwilling to listen or understand the pain, you instead explain why it happened. You may be thinking that *understanding why will make the pain go away. It won't. They just need their feelings heard.*

7. **Sparring.** This is a listening block. The person in pain can't be heard because you're ready to debate or disagree with what they say. By concentrating on verbal jabs the speaker can't be heard because you're not listening.

If you were able to identify with one or two of these communication mistakes, congratulations. Knowing your defense will help you pause the next time you're tempted to use it. *Wondering what to do instead?*

Let's move to the next tool, the **Compassionate Listening Recipe.**

We all have times when other people's pain makes us feel uncomfortable. That's often the reason we automatically reach for one of the common defenses listed previously. Those are ways to do something to brush away our discomfort. *How can we turn our hearts to a more compassionate stance to a person in pain?* Take a breath and bring all your attention to the other person and let your ego concerns take a back seat for a while. *How can we show them we're interested in their feelings?* Look the person in the eye with warmth and an attitude of receptivity. Nod while they're sharing their feelings.

Here are specific steps to create a safe space for the person in pain to be heard:

1. Become aware of whatever defenses you may gravitate toward.
2. Put aside your discomfort by breathing slowly, listening to the speaker and letting them know you're interested in their feelings.
3. As you breathe slowly, your heart will open to a more receptive stance. Imagine receiving the speaker into your heart.
4. Next, **acknowledge the person's pain by paraphrasing back to them what you've heard them say**. For example, after a patient tells her surgeon that she's devastated by her pregnancy loss the doctor could say, "I hear that you're devastated by this loss, shocked, scared and broken hearted. I'm so sorry."
5. After the initial compassionate listening (acknowledging and paraphrasing feelings), you can offer some additional responses to attend to the person in pain. Other compassionate responses could involve offering **support** like, "How can I help you through this?" or asking

for the person to **elaborate** by saying something like, "Can you tell me more about it?" or **reducing isolation** by saying something like, "Together we can get through this."

APSERI – The Quick Way to Remember

Want a quick way to remember the five steps above? Just think **APSERI**

(Acknowledge and Paraphrase, Support, Elaborate, Reduce Isolation). You can write this acronym down before meeting with a person in pain if it helps you remember these parts of compassionate listening.

→ **A**cknowledge and **P**araphrase: "I hear you say…"
→ Offer **S**upport: "How can I help you through this?"
→ Ask them to **E**laborate: "Tell me more about this."
→ **R**educe **I**solation: "Together we can get through this."

Do's and Don'ts

As a therapist I've been called to tragedies to help survivors cope. Because of these experiences, I often teach people how to respond with compassion to others who are in pain. I was once asked to meet with a group of bank co-workers early on a Monday morning. Over the weekend, they had heard that one employee's boyfriend was killed in a motorcycle accident. When I met with them, they shared with me that they, "Don't know what to say to her" and expressed fear that they may say the wrong thing. I told them that saying, "I'm so sorry for your loss/pain/sorrow" is a very powerful balm when someone is overwhelmed with emotional pain. Here are some other quick do's and don'ts:

- DO: "I heard about your loss and I'm so sorry."
- DO: "If I can do anything to help you, let me know."
- DON'T: (dealing with death) "They're better off/in a better place."
- DON'T: (dealing with death) "It was his/her time."
- DON'T: (dealing with pain/loss) "This will make you stronger."

What to Say When You're the Source of Pain

It stinks, but at times each of us has been the source of someone else's pain. This is completely normal (we're all just human after all) and often the pain may not have been intentional. Yet it can be hard not to become defensive when we're being confronted about causing someone's pain.

But there is good news. Here's a technique you can use. When someone is angry at, afraid of or disappointed in you, they may criticize or blame you. How do you listen compassionately and help them without revving up your angry defenses?

If the Criticism is Valid, Acknowledge and Apologize

If we're at fault and the criticism is accurate and constructive, we can acknowledge and apologize. A heartfelt, **"I'm sorry"** goes a long way to recovering peace in damaged relationships. Sometimes our pride won't allow us to apologize. However, apologizing either for causing another's pain or saying, "I'm sorry" when others are in pain is very important and very powerful.

PRACTICE SAYING: "I'm sorry for hurting you."

Most of us find it unhelpful and annoying when the person who caused your pain won't own up to it. Also, just saying they're sorry for the pain existing may not feel like enough, especially if they're not sincere, which we can usually tell by listening to their tone of voice. If you *are* the cause, own up to it and sincerely apologize for hurting the person.

If The Criticism Feels Wrong/Misplaced:

We can apologize for causing others pain but what do we do when the criticism doesn't feel valid? That is trickier and takes more advanced skills. It's like an arrow coming right for you; you dodge it but still stay in the open with the archer.

The Covering Technique

What can you do when you get criticized? If the criticism is constructive, you can acknowledge it: "Yes, I did leave the lights on." But what about non-constructive criticism? If you disagree or just feel put down unfairly? How can you dodge the arrow and still stay open in that field with the archer who shot at you?

The Covering Technique lets you stay open while under attack by using the 3 P's of Agreement. First I'll explain and give examples of the 3 P's and then I'll offer a practice exercise.

Staying open while under attack includes using the 3 P's of Agreement. When we're criticized, we often want to immediately defend ourselves by denying the allegation. This is a normal human impulse and frequently hard to avoid. And our defense often closes the two-way communication. But sometimes we need to keep the communication going. *What can we do then?* When you notice the impulse to fight back, pause, take a breath and reach for one of these handy tools. Getting them in your brain now will make them available for when you might need them.

You may recognize the following agreement terms as they're used in many fields:

• Agreeing in Part
• Agreeing in Principle
• Agreement in Probability

Using the 3 P's keeps the dialogue open when you feel that the criticism may not be valid. It's an assertive way to find the grain of truth in the criticism while maintaining your perspective.

As an example, with couples or roommates there's usually one who has a higher standard of cleanliness. This can lead to conflict. For our cleanliness example, let's say George is accusing you and it's your job to use Covering with one or more of the 3 P's in order to stay in the conversation.

George says, "You never clean up your room. This place is a mess." Now people don't often change in their cleanliness standards much. But they still need a way to communicate openly. Let's take this common problem and use it to examine the three parts of Covering.

The Covering Technique has three parts:

1. *Agreeing in part* involves acknowledging the part of the criticism you agree with. "You're right, it has been a while since I cleaned up my room." Or "Sometimes (versus never) I let books and papers pile up in my room."
2. *Agreeing in probability* acknowledges there's chance the criticism is valid. "It's possible I haven't paid attention to cleaning lately." Or "You may be right that my room is a mess."
3. *Agreeing in principle* involves acknowledging that if the condition exists, the conclusion is likely. "It's true that if I never clean my room the place would be a mess." (This doesn't confirm or deny the condition).

I'll give more examples of the 3 P's of Agreement so you can get familiar with how they work. Let's start with staying open when you're criticized for arriving late for work.

Your boss says, "You're late for work again. You're disinterested and we can't tolerate that." Your response:

Agree in Part: (when criticism is partly true) "Yes, I sometimes find myself running late for work."

Agree in Probability: (there's a chance the criticism is valid) "You may be right that I have been running late and focusing on other things more than work lately."

Agree in Principle: (If the condition exists, then the conclusion is likely) "It's true that if I was disinterested in work I might show up late sometimes." Or "It's true that if I was running late it might show I was disinterested in my job."

In the previous case, the dialogue with the boss is still open and you weren't defensive. He may be open to hearing more from you and you created room to be in a better negotiating position.

Where have the 3 P's come from? Agreeing in part comes from the business world where it's called a "partial accord" meaning to agree on a portion of what's under dispute. Probability (or chance) comes from the field of mathematics and agreement in probability is used in psychology for negotiation. Agreeing in principle comes from the field of law as a stepping-stone to a contract.

Covering may be easier for some people who use arguments often like lawyers but practice can help all of us. It's good to practice Covering because when you're falsely accused you may feel angry and want to fight or you may hit a wall of shame and feel like shrinking away. If no dialogue comes to you because you feel too angry or ashamed, then use the Covering tool as it will at least keep the conversation flowing.

Another quick example:

Invalid criticism: "You're too uptight."

Response:

1. Agree in part: "*Sometimes* I get uptight when I'm anxious."
2. Agree in probability: "You *may be right*, I have been uptight recently."
3. Agree in principle: "It's *true, if* I am worried often, I'd be uptight often."

YOUR TURN TO PRACTICE THE COVERING TECHNIQUE

Take a moment to think of any criticism you received recently but that you think isn't valid. Create one or more agreements that could work.

Invalid criticism:_____

Response:

1. Agree in part_____
2. Agree in probability_____
3. Agree in principle_____

Recalling the key phrases may help, such as
- ➜ **"Sometimes…"**
- ➜ **"It's possible…"**
- ➜ **"If I…I'd be…"**

When you're feeling attacked, it's difficult to think clearly as we're wired to defend ourselves. So it's valuable to help your sluggish brain by having a tool to grab when you're pushed into a corner or being blamed. Covering may seem complicated and you may feel like a fencer at times working without skill just to keep the conversation flowing. But with a little practice, you'll be able to do it like a pro.

Take Aways:

1. The two types of anger are cold and warm. When you're in the zone of cold anger, you're most likely shut down and turned away from the person you're mad at. Communication is very difficult in the cold zone. When you're in the zone of warm anger, your heart has softened and you find you're more open to listening and sharing your thoughts and feelings. Communication is easier in the warm zone.

2. Use the "reaching for love" technique as a resource when coping with difficult people.

3. There are 7 Common Communication mistakes when it comes to listening to people in pain. Learning them can help you to avoid making these mistakes in sticky situations.

4. To aid in compassionate listening, become aware of your defenses, breathe slowly and imagine receiving the speaker into your heart.

5. For compassionate listening, practice APSERI:
   → Acknowledge,
   → Paraphrase,
   → Support,

→ Elaborate and

→ Reduce Isolation.

6. Practice and learn the power of sincerely saying, "I'M SORRY" in response to someone else's pain AND to apologize when you're the source of pain.

7. Covering by agreeing in part, probability or principle can be used to keep communication open when you feel that the criticism of you may not be valid.

CHAPTER ELEVEN

Grab Quick Communication Tips for Emergencies

Think of this chapter as your quick reference guide when you find yourself in a sticky situation or need help in a pinch. I'm going to introduce you to 19 delicate "how to" moments from how to deliver bad news to how to respond to rejection. The solutions are set out in a simple-to-view Do's and Don'ts format which is easy to read when you're in a hurry and need to grab a quick tool. You'll learn how to handle some challenging or emotionally charged conversations like a pro. We'll be using some of the tools that have been presented in the book and some new tools. For each of the 19 categories, I provide Do's and Don'ts plus examples and resources and I close with a bonus on digital etiquette. As a benefit, you'll gain confidence in your communication skills and have better relationships.

For maximum impact, we're going to return to one of our super tools: the 3- and 4-part messages.

Here's a quick reminder of the 3- and 4-part messages:

The 4-Part Message:
I notice…(facts, observations)
I think…(beliefs)
I feel…(my emotions)
I want…(actions)

The 3-Part Message
When you…(their behavior)
I feel… (my emotions)
I want/need…(action)

Ready to go? Let's dive in.

How to Deliver Bad News

When a moment like this arises, the danger involved is that you're about to deliver a shock to the other person's system. To help that person better absorb the shock, you'll want to offer a moment to prepare. Years ago, I was driving home from work when I got the call that my mother had died. I immediately found it hard to concentrate. I felt shaky and upset. Consequently, I had to pull over into some stranger's driveway to register the news. It took me a long while before I could even think of turning the car back on and continuing my drive home. Due to this experience, I learned a valuable lesson for when I deliver bad news. As the speaker, it's my job to make sure the listener is in a safe physical space (e.g. sitting down or in a stopped car). Once assured the person is safe, I deliver the news. Preparation, I've learned, is key.

- **DO**: Prepare the person: "I have important news... it's urgent you contact me (by phone) ... immediately (or at this time.)"

If it's not urgent, just bad news, you can say, "When it's convenient, please call me for some important news."

During the call make sure the person is in a safe place to hear the news. "Are you sitting down?" Or, "Are you driving? Can you pull over?"

Before you deliver the news, take a moment to steady your voice and to speak with compassion.

Then deliver the bad news. "Your father/mother just died. You didn't get into...school. You didn't get the job. You're being fired. The house fell out of escrow. Your car was broken into. Your tests came back and the result is..."

When Bad News Is Best Delivered in Person:

Ending of a personal relationship. Be direct.

- **DO**: Say something clear like, "I want to break up with you."

Pause for response.

Then tell why (whole message is best)

- **DON'T**: Blurt out bad news.
- **DO**: Take time to listen and allow for the reaction of the listener.

How to Approach a Boss for a Raise

- **DO**: Be assertive. "I would like to come to your office and talk to you. When are you available?" A 4-Part Whole Message is the most effective tool (see below)[1].

- **DON'T**: Pick a busy or inconvenient time or be too vague, passive or demanding. If you're too passive or aggressive, review Chapter Four on how to be assertive. Don't leave out any of the four parts of the whole message. Ask your boss to please hear you out before responding.

Example:

1. I've worked at this company for a year. All my evaluations have been stellar and my contract is up for renewal. I have other job options. I notice some others at my level are paid more than I make at this time (facts and observations only).

2. I think this company is a good fit for my skills and interests and I believe in loyalty. I think we're both benefitting (thoughts, beliefs, values).

3. I enjoy working here and with the people around me, including you. I like this company and would be sad if I left (emotions).

4. I want to ask you for a 20% raise of my current annual income. I would like your answer this week if possible. Thank you for considering my request (wants or needs).

---

[1] Whole messages consist of and are delivered in this order: facts, your thoughts, your feelings, your needs or wants. (See details and practice in Chapter Nine)

Allow for the Response

It's not only important to communicate clearly, it's also important to allow for a response. In a situation like the one above, make sure you've talked slowly enough to let your boss process the information. Then, after your 4-part message, wait and stay silent. Take a moment to look at your boss's face. Allow your request to be placed on the table and absorbed. Even if you're nervous, don't speak as it may dilute the strength of your full message. Paraphrase your boss's responses, breathe slowly and listen before reacting.

How to Approach Someone You're Attracted To

- **DO**: Use a 3-Part Message ("I notice...I feel...I want...").
- **DO**: Find something attractive or interesting about their appearance or behavior and make that your opening comment:
  1. "I noticed your yellow boots/bright smile/eyes twinkle" or, "When you walked into the room, I heard you laugh."
  2. "I feel like I want to get to know you better."
  3. "Can we chat now or meet later? /Or hang out?"
- **DON'T**: Tout your assets, brag or make lascivious sexual comments as opening statements. Don't criticize.

How to Deal with Your Shyness at a Party:

- **DO: Observe, Listen, Respond, Share, or use "OLRS"** to remember this order. As you enter the new venue, take the least threatening action to get warmed up to the situation like get a drink or some food. Then look around receptively, **observe** the room and zoom in on something in your environment you can comment about. Subtly **listen** to what others are talking about. **Respond** by chatting with someone standing or sitting near you about simple things like the food or décor. Keep the conversation going back and forth by asking questions such as, "How do you know the host?" and then **share** with how you know the host. If the conversation dies out after two or three back and forth exchanges, accept that and move on to another person and use the same conversational approach.

- **DO**: Practice a 3-part message to approach others. Even if you're more of a self-conscious wallflower, the 3-part, "I notice, I feel, I want" strategy will work to approach almost **anyone** at a gathering.

For example, let's say you take a seat at a table with strangers at an event.

"I <u>noticed</u> you ordered the chicken; is it good?"
"I <u>feel</u>…"(any self-disclosure; it doesn't have to be emotional) "excited to hear the speaker."
"I <u>want</u> to learn more about the subject."

Remember to allow a little quiet time to leave an opening for a response. Listen, then respond, then share.

In summary, how to start a conversation when shy:

- **DO**: Use the tool: **Observe, Listen, Respond, Share or use "OLRS"** if it helps you remember these steps.
- **DO**: Use the 3-part message (I notice, I feel, I want) as a conversation starter.
- **DON'T**: Sit by yourself expecting people to come to you. Be aware: If you've started to imagine that everyone at the party hates you or that you're superior or inferior to them, then your negativity bias (see Chapter Six) may have kicked in.
- **DO:** Check your anxiety level on a scale from low (0) to high (5). If your anxiety is high, proceed to the following breathing exercise.

Just Three Slow Breaths to Reduce the Anxiety of Shyness

Pause, focus on your body, look down and breathe slowly three times. On the inhalation, concentrate on the sensation of the air in your throat, then chest, then belly. Keep breathing in this manner until you feel calmer and more open to interaction. Next, look around slowly and smile softly. Look for something outside yourself that you can focus on, like watching a child play or listening to music, etc.

How to Deal with Grief and Loss: (theirs)

- **DO say this first:** "I'm so very sorry for your loss and I'd like to offer my condolences. Is there anything I can do for you at this time of sorrow?" (Share condolences, offer support.)
- **DON'T let the first thing you tell them be:** "It was God's will" or "The deceased is better off

now" because regardless of faith, at a time of death this kind of sentiment can feel minimizing to the bereaved. If you're unsure what to do, take a breath, listen and follow the person's lead. Just being an unafraid witness (listening without judgment or a need to go anywhere) can be very healing for the person in pain.

How to Deal with People Who Are in a Rage
- **DO**: Start by deciding to use a calming tone of voice. Then, use this version of a 3-part message: "When you... I feel... and I want/need..."

For example, "*When you* raise your voice and talk in that tone to me, I *feel* scared, I find I want to shrink away and then I get mad, feel defensive and can't hear what you're saying to me. I understand you're upset but I *need* you to lower your voice. If you can't, I *want* you to stop and take a break so we can talk later when you're less upset." Your choice to use a calming tone may help bring the other person down from anger. This can help someone go from the RED zone to the GREEN zone (as explored in Chapter Three). If that fails, create a physical separation.

- **DON'T**: Amp up, start yelling or meet the other person at the same high level of rage.
- **DON'T**: Argue with someone who's been drinking or using drugs. Their mood is affected by these substances. They won't be able to be reasonable. If they're in a rage and you want to engage with them,

you can ask them to contact you when they're sober.

- **DO heed this warning: Getting away physically is primary if you feel scared that your physical safety is in danger.**

How To Manage Your Rage

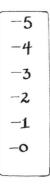

- **DO**: Check your anger level on the thermometer (5 is high, 0 is non-existent).

Take a moment to notice how you're currently breathing. Take five slow breaths, counting to four on the inhale and seven on the exhale. This will help you to down regulate (bring your anger down) quickly. Check the thermometer once again. What number are you at now? If the number is still high, breathe again or walk away, close your eyes (to calm down) or take a moment apart from others to scream (if safe to do so) to discharge any excess anger in your body. Check the thermometer again.

- **DO:** Move away from the scene of rage if you find you can't calm down. If safe to do so, lock yourself away in your room or bathroom or leave the house or area. Engage in either calming (meditating) or safe discharging (go for a run).
- **DON'T**: Go after someone when you're in a rage. Don't escalate the situation by engaging. The impulse to fight must be resisted when you're too hot to think clearly.
- **DO:** Take a time-out until you cool down. Exercise may help. Only when you're calmer should you talk to others about the conflict. If you're not calm, say something like, "I think I need some more time to calm down; we can talk later."
- **DON'T**: Engage in the subject of the conflict when you're in a rage. Your brain on rage will only be able to see bad and good, wrong and right, with no capacity for empathy, understanding or compromise. (For details see "your brain on rage" in Chapter Four.)

How to Stand Up for Your Needs
- **DO:** Be assertive.

EXAMPLE: Returning rotten fruit to a store

Assertive: "I need you to refund me for this rotten fruit."

- **DON'T**: Be passive, aggressive or passive-aggressive.

EXAMPLE: (Talking to a clerk after having bought rotten fruit at a store.)

Passive: "I don't want to bother you. I'm sorry, never mind, I guess I can still eat this fruit."

Aggressive (bullying): "Are you kidding me? What kind of a place is this that would sell rotten fruit? Don't you even check it? You people are incompetent. Give me my money back right now, you idiot!"

Passive-Aggressive (behaving in a hostile way without owning up to your anger directly): "I guess I can eat around the rotten parts. I hope I don't get sick."

How to Deal with People in Pain

Example: Interacting with someone who's severely ill or in an emergency room.

- **DO**: Realize they're scared and usually anxious due to their pain.
- **DO**: Listen; **DO**: Offer comfort; **DO**: Reassure; **DO**: Ask what they need.
- **DON'T**: Minimize their pain. **DON'T**: Tell them it could be worse (it could *ALWAYS* be worse; however, that information may just scare the person more) **DON'T**: Impose religious views or offer prayers unless they request it.

How to Cope with Sadness or Depression (theirs)

- **DO:** Express empathy by saying something like, "I see you're feeling down. I'm sorry you're so low. Can I help in some way? I'm here to listen." CAUTION: If your friend is suicidal and has a suicide action plan, seek help or call an emergency crisis hotline such as 1-(888) 724-7240 (available seven days a week, 24 hours a day) for immediate help; for medical emergencies call 911 in the USA. Check if these numbers are still active.

- **DON'T**: Ignore or minimize signs of sadness or depression. For example, "Get over it!" or "Just snap out of it!"
- **DON'T**: Blame or shame them. For example, don't say, "You brought this on yourself " (blame) or "You're a worthless sad sack" (shame).

How to Cope with Sadness or Depression (yours)

- **DO**: Say something like, "When you offer comfort, I appreciate it. I feel like… being alone/not going out/hunkering down/a bowl of soup/ a hug would help. Please… just sit quietly in the same room with me/leave me alone for a while/bring me some water/tell me a story/read to me." (In other words, decide what you most want and ask for it.)
- **DON'T**: Isolate for too long. When guilt or loneliness creeps in or if your anxiety gets high, you're in danger of circling the drain. When you notice you may be sinking deeper into depression, REACH out to someone. If you feel SUICIDAL, call for help. In the USA call 911 (USA emergency line) or 1-(800) 273-8255, the USA National Suicide Prevention Lifeline and get immediate help. www.suicidepreventionlifeline.org.

How to Manage Fear (yours)

- **DO:** Assess the *actual* over the imagined threat or danger. (Ask yourself, is it possible that I'm NOT in danger?) Be compassionate by realizing your body is responding biologically to some sense of danger. Look for ways to increase your sense of safety in the environment.
- **DO:** Communicate your fear if you're with a trusted person.
- **DO:** Ask for external help, support or protection if available. If you don't know who to reach out to, consider a warm line or a hotline. A warm line is for people struggling with mental health dealing with anxiety or depression. The aim of the warm line is to provide a reassuring voice for people before they reach a point of crisis. It's run by peers who often have had their own struggles and are there to mostly listen. A list of warm lines by US states can be found at www.warmline.org.
- **DO:** Manage your fear with internal resources like breathing and recalling your strengths and talents, thinking of someone you love or imagining being in a safe place. If possible, create a place that feels safe (like crawling onto a cozy couch with a warm blanket).

How to Manage Fear (theirs)

- **DON'T**: Go further into a risky or dangerous situation (if you have a choice) until you feel confident you're willing to risk the danger for the potential reward.

- **DO:** Use a 3-part message (I see, I feel, I want). For example: "I see you look a little scared; I feel protective of you; I want to help you feel safer. Would a hug help? Shall I go in first? Can I hold your hand?"

How to Handle Rejection (yours: when you're rejected)

- **DO:** Deliver the entire (4-part) whole message, ideally in person. Example:
  1. (Facts) "When you said our relationship was over, I went into shock and couldn't believe it and couldn't say anything but now I'm able to."
  2. (Values) "I believed in our commitment to fidelity."
  3. (My emotions now) "I feel betrayed, enraged and distraught."
  4. (Want or need) "I want to hurt you back so badly but I won't. I need you to stay away from me."
- **DON'T:** Lash out in rage.
- **DON'T:** Look for something or someone else to blame like the betrayer's new crush, their job, family or friends. Keep the focus on your response to that person's behavior.

How to Handle Rejection (theirs: when you're rejecting)

- **DO:** Deliver a 3-part break-up message (when you...I feel...I want...) Example:

1. When you talked about wanting to flirt with other people,
2. I felt my heart sink, realizing you wouldn't stay faithful to me.
3. I want to break up with you even though it breaks my heart.

- **DON'T:** Take responsibility for their feeling of rejection.

Reacting In Cases of Boredom, Insult, Oppression or Abuse: How to SET BOUNDARIES

How to Respond When You're Bored or Not Interested:

- **DO:** Politely cut them off mid-sentence: "I'm so sorry. You've told me this story before. I <u>need</u> to go back to work/cooking/driving/an appointment now or I'll be late."
- **DON'T:** Tell them how you really feel as this can be needlessly hurtful. For example, don't say, "When you talk about... I find it boring and don't want to hear you talk anymore. Please be quiet." This has the possibility of closing all contact.
- **DO:** Try to change the subject to something of mutual interest: "Tell me about your/your child's/your grandchild's baseball game."

How to Respond to Being Insulted:

- **DO:** Notice and register what's going on inside your body like where you're feeling the insult (or pain) and how it feels. For example, if your fists are balling up and your heart is racing, you're likely feeling angry. If your throat tightens, heart sinks and eyes sting, you may feel hurt. If you get light-headed and spacey, you may feel shocked. Pay attention to how your body is affected by the insult. Breathe into your body before deciding how to respond.

- **DO:** Respond using this format: (When you/I feel/and I want/)

  1. "When you (repeat insult) call me selfish and tell me I care more about work/money/myself more than I care about you,

  2. I feel hurt, angry and misunderstood and I feel compelled to defend myself.

  3. I want you to stop insulting me and stick to the issue (e.g. my unwillingness to travel to your graduation) not my personality."

- **DO:** Imagine you have an armored breast plate and a hand out in front of you with your hand at 90 degrees like a "stop" gesture.

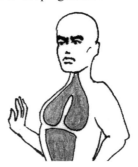

Inhale. On the exhale practice saying, "No" in a low loud voice. Practice this "No" with the "stop" gesture over and over to build a sense of momentum and power. Once you feel grounded in your strength, you can approach the other person.

- **DON'T:** Be passive aggressive (an indirect expression of hostility used to hurt the person as a way to avoid setting a boundary). Some examples are sullen behavior (acting subtly grumpy, sulky or gloomy) or failing to finish required tasks on purpose.

How to React When You Feel Oppressed:
Warning: Oppression (being pressured) can turn into abuse when it crosses a line into some physical action like being pushed, shoved or hit.

- **DO:** Say, "I feel forced/pushed/pressured and I don't like that feeling. Stop intruding on my right to (for example) eat what I want."
- **DON'T:** Submit for the sake of peace if you're really bothered.

How to React When You're in An Abusive Moment:
- **DO:** Say, "I experience you as abusive and will not tolerate being treated that way. Stop or leave."
- **DO:** (Option) physically leave the area by yourself if you can do so safely.
- **DON'T:** Submit to abuse unless rebellion feels too threatening for you to tolerate or manage. If your life is in danger or feels like it could be, do

whatever you deem the smartest way to stay alive in the moment.

- **DO:** Get professional help if you can't get away physically or emotionally from an abuser.
- **DO:** In cases of severe or chronic abuse, de-escalate the danger in whatever way necessary (e.g. cooperation or submission) until you feel safe enough to get away or seek outside help. (current USA National Domestic Abuse Hotline: 1- (800) 799-7233.)
- **DON'T:** Let shame or dependence on the abuser stop you from seeking help.

CAUTION: In cases of severe abuse you may want to de-escalate the potential or actual abuse in whatever way necessary until you can physically get away. When you can't escape and must tolerate abuse, your body finds ways to cope such as spacing out. Appreciate the body's ability to do this, as sometimes the only escape is into an internal world of your own. No one deserves abuse but if you can't escape or are too scared to attempt it, please seek outside help as there are many trained therapists available to assist you.

BONUS!
A Few Quick Notes on Digital Etiquette
In our current world landscape, we have multiple options when we want to communicate. We can text, email, call, video chat or see someone in person. There's no doubt about it, the digital world is swiftly changing our communication habits. There are no hard and fast rules for digital etiquette. However,

generally the rule is: *the more you're concerned about being misunderstood, the more personal the contact should be.* So consider how high the stakes are in each situation before choosing your communication platform.

Digital Communication Levels
Though we may not think about it on a regular basis, within our digital communication are levels of personalization. Let's examine a few of them.

1. **Least personal:** Email and text. (Why? Because there's no voice tone, therefore it's not good for emotionally laden communication due to high chances for misunderstandings.)
   - **DON'T:** Email or text when the emotional content of your communication is crucial.

2. **More personal:** Calling has voice; video chat (online view and sound) has voice and the person's face. Seeing someone's expressive face in real time can make you feel closer to them or can help you understand them better.

3. **Most personal:** In person (live) is the most intimate and best for subtle communication nuances. It affords the best chances for spontaneity. It's the only method with an opportunity for physical contact and maneuvering in the same physical space. When you want to have a personal talk about something important, you should gently request that mobile devices be turned off.

Take Aways:

1. When delivering bad news, don't just blurt it out. Prepare the listener and make sure they're safe physically before you share the information.

2. When starting a conversation, if you're shy use "OLRS" (*Observe, Listen, Respond, Share*).

3. Using a 3- or 4-part message ("I notice...I think...I feel...I want...") can be helpful when
   - Approaching someone you're attracted to
   - Asking for a raise
   - You feel shy
   - You're dealing with someone who's in a rage
   - You're responding to being insulted
   - Handling rejection

4. When dealing with a person who's sad or depressed, express empathy and ask if you can help. Don't minimize, blame or shame. If they're suicidal, seek professional help and call 911 (USA only) or a suicide hotline.

5. When coping with your own sadness or depression, ask for what you need. Be careful not to isolate for too long. If you feel SUICIDAL, call for help. In the USA call 911 (USA emergency line) or a suicide hotline and get immediate help.

6. When managing your fears assess the *actual* over the imagined threat or danger. Use self-soothing skills to calm your nerves.

7. When managing the fears of others, don't go further into a risky or dangerous situation. Do use a 3-part message (when you...I feel...I want).

8. In cases of oppression, abuse or boredom, learn how to set boundaries.

9. When you're the victim in an abusive moment, state your experience and that you will not tolerate being treated that way. Say, "Stop or Leave." Don't submit to abuse UNLESS rebellion feels too threatening for you to tolerate or manage. If your life is in danger or feels like it could be, do whatever you deem the smartest way to stay alive in the moment.

10. When standing up for your needs, use assertiveness skills and avoid passiveness, aggressiveness or passive-aggressiveness.

11. When someone is in pain, do your best to listen, be present and avoid minimizing the situation.

12. When you feel you've been insulted, notice how your body is affected. Breathe before deciding how to respond.

13. Within digital communication are three levels of personalization. Email and text can't convey emotional content well. Calling and video chat add visual and voice prosody. Understanding the limits of each type of digital format can help you avoid miscommunication.

Closing Summary

I created this book to offer you, my reader, an innovative approach to communication. Combining the latest in brain science with techniques that encourage you to listen to your body, my hope is that your relationships will be transformed by improved communication.

Along this journey, I hope you've plucked a few fabulous flowers that either filled your body with a scent that shifted your mood so you can communicate more effectively, or that filled your brain with the beauty of many quick communication tools to grab in a moment of need.

Don't be afraid to re-read the tools, rehearse with a trusted friend or be honest with your communication partner as you hone your skills. Keep this book by your bedside the night before you intend to communicate something important to your partner, child, co-worker or boss. Read it right before you head off to speak to a relative in pain or before you approach a new crush.

In my experience, I've found that it takes practice to use these tools successfully. Don't worry if some tools don't work the first time. For the most part, people want to understand us. So, try again. When you experience that first moment of communication success, you'll fill with newfound confidence. I've watched it happen many times and I never tire seeing people discover triumphant new ways to feel heard and understood.

It's simple. And it's transformative. Better communication makes for better relationships and therefore a better life!

Resources and Notes

1 – Your Hard-Wired Brain and Talking Body Help Communication

Lowen, A. (1976). *Bioenergetics*. New York: MacMillan Publishing Co.

Porges, S. (2011). *The Polyvagal Theory: Neuropsychological Foundations of Emotions, Attachment, Communication, & Self-Regulation*. New York: Norton.

Schroeter, V. (2016). "Polyvagal theory: An Introduction for Somatic Psychotherapy." *Bioenergetic Analysis, Clinical Journal of the IIBA*. Vol. 26: 9-40.

Siegel, D., and Bryson, T. (2011). *The Whole Brain Child*. New York: Delacorte Press.

2 – Listening Blocks and Assertiveness Issues that Get in your Way

Alberti, R. E., and Emmons, M. (2017). *Your Perfect Right.* 10th ed. San Luis Obispo, CA: Impact Press. NOTE: First published 1970, contains the origin of assertive, passive and aggressive styles.

Barker, L. L. (1990). *Listening Behavior.* New Orleans: Spectra. (active listening clarified)

Davis, M., Paleg, K., & Fanning, P. (2004). *The Messages Workbook.* Oakland, CA: New Harbinger publications. NOTE: This book contains many listening practice exercises.

Gordon, T. (1962). *Parent Effectiveness Training.* New York: Random House, Inc. NOTE: Although many therapy systems (like CBT and DBT) refer to 10 listening blocks, they likely originated from Thomas Gordon's "12 roadblocks" to communication, created in 1957.

Helms M. M., and Haynes P. J. (1992). "Are You Really Listening?: The Benefit Of Effective Intra-Organizational Listening." *Journal of Managerial Psychology*, Vol. 7 (6): 17-21. NOTE: Resource for active vs. pseudo-listening.

McKay, M., Davis, M., & Fanning, P. (1995). *Messages.* Oakland, CA: New Harbinger publications. NOTE: This book states the four intentions of real listening.

3 – Mastering your Breath is the Secret Weapon That Can Change Your Moods

Corrigan, F. M., Fisher, J. J., Nutt, D. J. (2010). "Autonomic dysregulation and the Window of Tolerance model of the effects of complex emotional trauma. *Journal of Psychopharmacology.* Vol. 25 (1)17-25.

Lowen, A. (1977). *The Language of the Body.* New York: Mac-Millan Publishing Co.

Lowen, A., and Lowen, L. (1977). *The Way to Vibrant Health.* New York: Harper Calophon Books.

Ogden, P., Minton, K., & Pain, C. (2006). *Trauma and the Body: A Sensorimotor Approach to Psychotherapy.* New York: W.W. Norton.

Porges, S. (2011). *The Polyvagal Theory: Neurophysiological Foundations of Emotions, Attachment, Communication, and Self-Regulation.* (Norton series on Interpersonal Neurobiology). New York: W.W. Norton & Company.

Schroeter, V. (2009). *Character Armoring: Walls Between Oneself and the World.* In book: Revelation of the Breath: a tribute to its power, wisdom and beauty. Ed. Sharon Mijares. New York: Suny Press.

Schroeter, V., and Thomson, B. (2011). *Bend Into Shape: Techniques for Bioenergetic Therapists.* Psychosozial Verlag.

4 – Discover the Tricks to Becoming More Assertive

Schroeter, V., and Thomson, B. (2011). *Bend Into Shape: Techniques for Bioenergetic Therapists.* Giessen: Psychosozial Verlag.

Siegel, D. (2010). *Mindsight.* New York: Bantam Books. NOTE: This book is the resource for the brain on rage.

Siegel, D., & Bryson, T. (2011). *The Whole Brain Child.* New York: Random Publishing Group. NOTE: This book is the resource for "name it to tame it" exercise.

5 – Train Your Brain to Become the Best Listener Ever

Cozolino, L. (2016). *Why Therapy Works.* New York: W.W. Norton &Co. Inc.

Levine, P. (1997). *Waking the Tiger – Healing Trauma.* Berkeley, CA: North Atlantic Books.

McKay, M., Davis, M., & Fanning, P. (1995). *Messages: The Communication Skills Book.* Oakland,CA: New Harbinger Publications, Inc.

Newton, R. P. (2017). *Scaffolding the brain: A neurobiological approach to observation, assessment and intervention. Parts A & B.* Integrative Regulation Therapy (iRT*).* Unpublished manuscript.

Rosenberg, M. (2015). *Non-violent Communication.* Encinitas, CA: Puddle Dancer Press.

Schroeter, V. (2014). "Integration of Regulation Therapy and Bioenergetic Analysis," *Bioenergetic Analysis, Clinical Journal of the IIBA.* Vol. 24: 105-132.

Van Der Kolk, B., (2015). *The Body Keeps the Score.* New York: Penguin Books.

6 - Gain Mastery at Listening to Difficult People

Hanson, R. and Mendius, R. (2009). *Buddha's Brain, The practical neuroscience of happiness, love and wisdom.* Oakland, CA: New Harbinger Publications, Inc. p.48.

Lowen, A. (1975). *Bioenergetics.* New York: Penguin Compass.

7 – Become Understood by Expressing Your Feelings with New Clarity

Jourard, S.M. (1971). *The Transparent Self: Self-Disclosure and Well-Being.* New York: Van Nostrand Reinhold. NOTE: Resource of "I" messages and self-disclosure.

Lowen, A. (1980). *Fear of Life.* New York: Collier Books.

Schroeter, V., and Thomson, B. (2011). *Bend Into Shape*: *Techniques for Bioenergetic Therapists.* Giessen: Psychosozial Verlag.

Schroeter, V. (2013). "Movement Through Grief." Keynote address, Southern California Bioenergetic Conference, Lake Arrowhead, CA. Unpublished manuscript.

8 – Your Voice and a Pillow: The Cure for Stuffing Emotions

Lowen, A. (1995). *Joy, The Surrender to the Body and to Life.* New York: Penguin Compass,

Schroeter, V. and Thomson, B.(2011). *Bend Into Shape: Techniques for Bioenergetic Therapists.* Giessen: Psychosozial Verlag.

9 – The Magic Power of Whole Messages

Gordon, T. (1970). *Parent Effectiveness Training.* New York: Random House, Inc.

McKay, M., Davis, M., & Fanning, P. (1995). *Messages.* Oakland, CA: New Harbinger Publications. NOTE: I learned about whole messages from the book *Messages*. Here's some of the history. John Dewey (1859-1952) was an American philosopher who created a 6-step "reflective thinking" problem-solving model. Sidney Jourad (1926-1974) was a Canadian psychologist who introduced the value of self-disclosure using "I" statements in communication. Thomas Gordon (1918-2002) was an American clinical psychologist, widely recognized as a pioneer in teaching communication skills. Gordon added some of Dewey's material to his relational model in 1962. Jourad's "I" messages were added to Gordon's PET (parent effectiveness model) model in his book for parents (1970). Michael E. Cavanagh (1980) combined some of these ideas in his book *Make Your Tomorrow Better.* M. McKay, M. Davis and P. Fanning in their book *Messages* (1995) refer to Cavanagh, Gordon, Jourad and Cavanagh in influencing the whole messages model. Linda Adams

(1976) in working with parents came up with a 3-part message related to self-disclosure. She said it's declarative (when you - I think), responsive (I feel) and preventive (I want). She renamed the 3-part message "The confrontive 'I' message."

Rosenberg, M. (2015). *Non-Violent Communication.* 3rd edition. Encinitas, CA: Puddle Dancer Press.

10 – Ways to Stay Open in Order to Get through Conflict

Lowen, A. (1995). *Joy: Surrender to the Body and to Life.* New York: Penguin Compass.

Smith, M.J. (1975). *When I say no, I feel guilty.* New York: Bantam Books.

Thich Nhat Hanh. (1991). *Peace is Every Step.* New York: Bantam Books.

11 – Grab Quick Communication Tips for Emergencies

Lowen, A. (1995). *Joy, The Surrender to the Body and to Life.* New York: Penguin Compass.

Schroeter, V. (2000). "The Grief of Infertility: one therapist's journey." In book: *Body Psychotherapy in Progressive and Chronic Disease,* ed. Christa Ventling. Basel: Karger Books.

Acknowledgements and Credits

I want to thank my writing coach, Marni Freedman, who has shepherded this book from the beginning with tenacity and talent. Once we had the book in an acceptable form, it took an army of professionals to get it in shape for publishing. I give credit to Jason Warren, graphic artist, who prepared the sketches that I drew, adapted them for print and edited the cover. Andrea Glass and Lynette Smith were generous in sharing information and highly experienced in copyediting, layout and proofreading. Thank you to the interior formatting and publishing team of Marijke McCandless and Danielle White and to Garry Cockburn for proofreading. Buzbooks transformed my ideas into a beautiful cover design. Finally, I want to thank my family and friends for their ongoing love and support during this journey. Thank you, siblings Ken, Peggy, Bonny, Sean, Cefe, Maria, Josefa, Kevin, Peter, Anita and Rick. Thank you to my daughter Rayna and her family Geoff, Hayden and Harrison and to my friends Tarra, Golda, Carole and George. Finally, thanks to Steve, my husband and life partner, for his technical and emotional support at every step along the way.

ABOUT THE AUTHOR

Vincentia Schroeter, PhD, has practiced psychotherapy for over forty years, specializing in addictions, attachment and Bioenergetic Analysis. She has written extensively on somatic psychotherapy and has been published in professional journals and books. She co-wrote *Bend Into Shape: Techniques for Bioenergetic Therapists* with co-author Barbara Thomson in 2011. She is on the international faculty of the IIBA, teaching Bioenergetics locally and around the world. Her studies in self-psychology, affect regulation and interpersonal neurobiology have influenced her counseling methods.
Website: Vincentiaschroeterphd.com

Made in the USA
Columbia, SC
07 December 2018